QUIET
ONE YEAR DAIL
for Children in GRADES 5-6

CHAMPION

Quiet Time
One year daily devotional for children in grades 5-6

Published by Word of Life Local Church Ministries
A division of Word of Life Fellowship, Inc.

Joe Jordan - Executive Director
Jack Wyrtzen & Harry Bollback - Founders
Mike Calhoun - VP of Local Church Ministries

USA
P.O. Box 600
Schroon Lake, NY 12870
1-888-932-5827
talk@wol.org

Canada
RR#8/Owen Sound
ON, Canada N4K 5W4
1-800-461-3503 or (519) 376-3516
lcm@wol.ca

Web Address: www.wol.org

Publisher's Acknowledgements
Writers and Contributors: Betsi Calhoun, Beverly Deck, Amy Speck
Editor: Betsi Calhoun
Curriculum Manager: Don Reichard
Cover Design: Solo Multimedia, Inc.
Page layout and design: Beth Shoultz

ISBN - 978-1-931235-50-1
Printed in the United States of America

GOD LOVES YOU
& wants to spend time
WITH YOU

Quiet Time is a special time that you set aside each day to read God's Word to get to know Him better and to learn how He wants you to live. During this time, God speaks to you through His Holy Word the Bible and you speak to God through prayer. As a Christian, spending this time everyday is very important for you to grow closer to God.

The Champion Quiet Time will help you have a special time each day with the Lord. This booklet is divided into two sections. A Personal Prayer Diary section where you can write prayer requests to remind yourself to pray for people that you care about and things that are happening. The second section is the Quiet Time Activity Pages. Activities are written from the Bible verses for each day of the year to challenge you to understand the truths from God's Word.

The Champion Quiet Time and the Teen/Adult Quiet Times use the same Scriptures for the week. This makes it easier for your whole family to discuss the passages together.

a note to parents:

This Quiet Time is a great opportunity for you to have fun together with your child. Here are some tips to help your child with their Quiet Time.

>> Gather supplies needed for activities.

>> Sit down at a prescribed time each day.

>> Use the Bible to look up references together.

>> Talk through the activity and personal application.

>> Complete the enrichment activity together (it is written to you the parent).

>> Help your child complete the Christian Service projects and help get their friends involved also!

>> Complete the week by documenting how many days were completed and writing an encouraging note.

your daily quiet time

Begin the week by reading the overview. This will give you a hint about what you will learn that week. Extra facts will increase your understanding of the week's passage.

Each day, read the Daily Scripture Passage.

Complete the activity for the day.

Write down your prayer requests in your diary and talk to God in prayer.

Suggested Christian Service Activities are highlighted each week for you to serve God by serving others.

wk. 1

Chart YOUR Course

WEEKLY PASSAGES COVERED
Psalm 104:1-105:45

Did you know there are five whole books of poetry in the Bible?

Can you number these in the order they appear in God's Word?

PSALMS # _____

JOB # _____

ECCLESIASTES # _____

PROVERBS # _____

SONG OF SOLOMON # _____

SUNDAY — Psalm 104:1-13

take the challenge

CHECK IT OUT

Have you ever gone outside at night and looked up at the hundreds of stars in the sky? What kind of questions does that cause you to wonder about the Creator of the universe?

All the things we read about God the Creator and Sustainer of nature back up verse one: "_____ the _____, O my _____. O _____ my God, Thou art very _____.
Thou art clothed with _____ and _____."

1} _____

2} _____ (v.3)

3} _____ (v.5)

_____ (v.10)

make YOUR choice

I will BLESS or HONOR my Creator today by . . .

_____

Things needed for my Quiet Time:

>> Bible   >> Quiet Time

>> Pen   >> A quiet place

4

Keeping a Personal Prayer Diary is a great way to remind yourself to pray for specific people and things. It also reminds you to thank God and to tell others when He answers your prayers.

Your prayer time should include praying for friends and family. Especially pray for those who don't know Christ as their Savior.

You should also pray for your Christian friends, your relatives and yourself. Pray that you will grow in your Christian life and become what God wants you to be.

Get to know missionaries who serve the Lord in your area or around the world. Ask them for specific prayer requests. Write these on your prayer pages.

Much of your prayer time should be used thanking and praising God. Tell God that you are thankful for your salvation, parents, home, friends, and answers to prayers.

You should praise God for His beautiful creation, His holiness and His greatness.

Some prayer time should include asking God to meet needs such as clothing, food or maybe a job for your dad. Maybe you could ask God to help you be more obedient. You must be careful not to be selfish and ask for things that you want only for you. As you are obedient to God, He will care for your needs.

My personal PRAYER diary . . .

Daily prayer requests are those things that you pray for each day. Maybe someone in your family will be traveling one day and you ask God to protect them as they travel. For each request, write the date that you started praying for it and how God answered your prayer.

daily prayer requests

name **date** **how God answered**

....

....

....

....

....

....

....

....

....

....

....

....

....

....

name   **date**   how God answered

....

....

....

....

....

....

....

....

....

....

....

....

....

....

....

....

....

....

....

weekly prayer request

The Weekly Prayer Request Chart can be used to remind you to pray for specific requests either once a week or more often. Write down the names of friends and family members. Don't forget to include those that need to be saved. Put the names of your church leaders and missionaries that you know so that you can remember to pray for them as well. For each request, write the date that you started praying and how God answered your prayer.

SUNDAY

family & friends

name	date	how God answered

missionaries & church leaders

I THANK God for . . .   I PRAISE God for . . .

8

family & friends

name   date   how God answered

missionaries & church leaders

I THANK God for . . .   **I PRAISE God for . . .**

family & friends

name · date · · · how God answered

missionaries & church leaders

I THANK God for . . .   **I PRAISE God for . . .**

family & friends

name   date   how God answered

missionaries & church leaders

I THANK God for . . .   I PRAISE God for . . .

family & friends

name   date   how God answered

missionaries & church leaders

I THANK God for . . .   I PRAISE God for . . .

family & friends

name   date   how God answered

....

....

....

....

....

....

....

....

....

missionaries & church leaders

....

....

....

....

I THANK God for . . .   I PRAISE God for . . .

....

....

....

....

family & friends

name   date   how God answered

missionaries & church leaders

I THANK God for . . .   **I PRAISE God for . . .**

Christian Service Activities

The following is a list of Christian Service Activities for you to learn how to serve God by serving others. A more detailed explanation of each activity is available in the Word of Life Olympian Christian Service Manual. To order yours, contact Local Church Ministries at

1.888.932.5827

Encouragement Ministry Opportunities

ICS - 1 . . . . Encouragement Cards
ICS - 2 . . . . Get Well Card
ICS - 3 . . . . Giving Thanks
ICS - 4 . . . . Helping Hands At Home
ICS - 5 . . . . Ministry Of Helps
ICS - 6 . . . . . Ministry To College Student
ICS - 7 . . . . Ministry To Elderly
ICS - 8 . . . . Missionary Letter
ICS - 9 . . . . Pray For An Adult
ICS - 10 . . . . Pray With A Friend
ICS - 11 . . . . Telephone Ministry
ICS - 12 . . . . Thank You Letter

Church or Evangelistic Opportunities

ICS - 13 . . . . Absentee Visitation
ICS - 14 . . . . Create A Tract
ICS - 15 . . . . Evangelistic Highlight
ICS - 16 . . . . Family Devotions
ICS - 17 . . . . Gospel Tracts
ICS - 18 . . Help A Sunday School Teacher
ICS - 19 . . . . Help Church Secretary
ICS - 20 . . . . . . Help In The Nursery
ICS - 21 . . . . Invite A Friend
ICS - 22 . . . . Pen Pal
ICS - 23 . . . . Prayer Partner Card
ICS - 24 . . . . Puppet Ministry
ICS - 25 . . . . Servant's Heart
ICS - 26 . . . . Special Music
ICS - 27 . . . . Tell A Friend
ICS - 28 . . . . . . Testimony By Olympian
ICS - 29 . . . . Visitation
ICS - 30 . . Testimony By Coach Or Parent

Encouragement Ministry Opportunities

GCS - 1 . . . . Boxes Of Blessing
GCS - 2 . . . . Church Clean-up
GCS - 3 . . Clean & Decorate Olympian Rm.
GCS - 4 . . . . Food Pantry
GCS - 5 . . . . Flower Garden
GCS - 6 . . . . Get Well Cards
GCS - 7 . . . . Ministry of Helps
GCS - 8 . . . . Pastor's Testimony
GCS - 9 . . . . Pray For Our Country
GCS - 10 . . . . Sharing From Plants
GCS - 11 . . . . Thank You Letters

Church or Evangelistic Opportunities

GCS - 12 . Christmas Or Holiday Caroling
GCS - 13 . . . . Drama Team
GCS - 14 . . . . Live Nativity
GCS - 15 . . . . Missionary Project
GCS - 16 . . . . Music Ministry
GCS - 17 . . . . Parade Float
GCS - 18 . . . . Project Prayer
GCS - 19 . . . . Puppet Ministry
GCS - 20 . . . . . Retirement Home Service
GCS - 21 . . . . . . Senior Citizens Group
GCS - 22 . . . . Tract Blitz
GCS - 23 . . . . Visit Shut-Ins
GCS - 24 . . . . . . Youth Emphasis Service

WK.

1

Temptation, Fear
Anxiety, Loneliness
& Gossip . . .

These are all things most people face on a daily basis. David faced these things too, and journalled his feelings in his diary as prayer songs or "psalms" to God. How did he deal with these feelings? Let's check it out this week!

SUNDAY Psalm 1:1-6

take the challenge

Did anyone ever say, "Bless you!" after you sneezed? What does it mean to be "blessed"?

CHECK IT OUT

Do you want to be blessed by God? He gives us three things NOT to do in these verses. Verse 1 says we should not w __ __ __ in the counsel of the ungodly (wicked), s __ __ __ __ (eth) in the way of sinners, or s __ __ in the seat of the scornful (mockers).

make your choice

What should I delight in according to verse 2?

_____

Who are the people in my life that I should spend time with and take advice from?_____

MONDAY Psalms 2:1-12

take the challenge

What foreign country would you most like to visit?

CHECK IT OUT

Verse 8 talks about the "uttermost part (or ends) of the earth." What do you think that means?_____ _____ How far away does God want His Word to be known and people to be saved?_____ _____

The last sentence in this psalm gives us a wonderful promise to claim: "Blessed are all who _____ _____."

make YOUR choice

Someday, all the peoples of the earth will have heard the gospel. Do I have a dream to take God's Word to a faraway land? _____ My dream mission field is _____.

TUESDAY Psalm 3:1-8

take the challenge

What would it be like to be surrounded by 10,000 soldiers?

CHECK IT OUT

When David wrote this psalm, he was surrounded by enemy soldiers, maybe as many as _____ (v. 6) of them! What does he say his enemies are doing in verse 1? _____ David felt alone and that everybody was against him... but he still had God on his side! In verses 3 and 8, he calls the Lord his _____ and the one Who gives _____ (v. 8).

make YOUR choice

When are some times that I feel alone or that no one cares? _____

Who is for me even when it feels like everyone else is against me?

_____ 17

WEDNESDAY Psalm 4:1-8

take the challenge

Monsters under my bed?

CHECK IT OUT

Are you ever afraid at night? Then verse 8 is for you! Write it on the lines below and then write it out on a card, put it under your pillow and claim it for your own as you go to bed tonight!

make YOUR choice

I can take time before I go to bed tonight to pray verse 8 as a prayer from my heart to God's!

thursday Psalm 5:1-12

take the challenge

"LIAR! LIAR! Pants on fire!"

CHECK IT OUT

Have you ever been called a liar or called someone else one? This passage describes liars. Fill in what each part of a liar is like according to verse 9

make YOUR choice

Look back at verse 3 to see how I can prepare my heart each day to be honest and true. How is my morning prayer time going these days?

friday Psalm 6:1-10

Do we always get what we deserve for our sin?

In this passage, David is lamenting (is sad about) his sin. Circle the symptoms of sin in his life (that are referred to in this chapter) below:

Felt afraid of God's anger - Felt faint and weak - Had the dry heaves
Felt like he was pining away - His bones even hurt - Had a lot of energy
Felt like having a party - His soul was anguished, vexed, dismayed
Was weary & tired from groaning & sighing - His eyes hurt
Flooded his bed with tears at night

Sometimes sinning sounds fun, but is it fun in the end? **Yes / No**

Write out David's grateful words from verse 9: _____
_____ Is there something for which I need
to ask God's forgiveness ? Write it here and then take time to talk to
God about it! _____

saturday Psalm 7:1-8

Have you ever had untrue things said about you?

David wrote this psalm because some people were saying untrue things about him...mainly that he was trying to kill King Saul and take over his throne. How did he describe these enemies of his in verse 2? _____
_____
_____ Whom did David talk to about
these untrue and hurtful sayings? Circle one: **friends**
- family - God - his dog - the mirror

Whom can I go to when someone has said hurtful things about me?
Unscramble: **SJSEU** _____ What can I do for the
person saying hurtful things? **YRPA** _____

19

Chart Your Course

2

David had lots of enemies on his heels when he was a young man.

Giant Goliath

King Saul

The Philistine Army

. . . Nabal, Abner, the Amalekites & Doeg

SUNDAY   Psalm 7:9-17

take the challenge

Can you believe it? My God knows all about me!

CHECK IT OUT

Verse 9 tells us that God knows what is in our hearts and minds. This can be comforting or worrisome, depending on what is in our minds! Below, make two lists. Write down three things that are good to think about and in the other list three things that we should not dwell on or think about.

Good Thoughts About:

_____
_____
_____

Bad Thoughts About:

_____
_____
_____

make your choice

How is my thought life? What can I do when bad thoughts enter my mind? Circle below (there are several right answers): **run away - pray and ask God for help - think on good things - be careful what I watch on TV - read good books - yell loudly**

MONDAY Psalm 8:1-9

take the challenge

Superman has nothing on my God!

CHECK IT OUT

Fill in the crossword puzzle below that has to do with things that God created that are written about in this psalm.

ACROSS
1) E _ _ _ _ (v.1)
2) B _ _ _ _ _ (v.7)
3) M _ _ (v.3)
4) S _ _ _ (v.3)

DOWN
5) M _ _ (v.4)
6) H _ _ _ _ _ _ (v.3)
7) How excellent (majestic) is Your N _ _ _ (v.9)
8) F _ _ _ (v.8)

make YOUR choice

Take time right now to fill in something you want to praise God for in your prayer pages. Then praise God for it! I praise God today for _____!

TUESDAY Psalm 9:1-10

take the challenge

Will my God stick with me through thick and thin?

CHECK IT OUT

Verse 9 tells us that the LORD is a _____ for those who are oppressed (or bullied around), especially in "times of _____." Verse 10 promises He has never _____ those who _____ Him. To "forsake" means to abandon. If you know Jesus as your Savior, He will never abandon you. You may experience hard things...but Jesus promises to be with you through it all. What two things should we do according to verse 10: T _ _ _ _ Him and S _ _ _ Him

make YOUR choice

What hard thing in my life do I want to give to Jesus?

_____

Take time now to talk to Him in prayer.

21

WEDNESDAY Psalm 9:11-20

take the challenge

Have you ever been to a real court and seen a case tried by a judge?

CHECK IT OUT

What does God never ignore or forget (v. 12)? _____ _____ Compare this to verse 18, which talks about God not forgetting the _____ or the _____. According to verse 16, the Lord is known by what? _____

"Justice" or "judgment" means to make fair decisions, giving people what they deserve for their actions.

make YOUR choice

As much as we try, we can never always be fair like God, because He is perfect. However, we can ask God to help us be fair in how we treat others. "Today, I want to be fair when I play with _____ _____. Jesus, please help me do this. Amen"

thursday Psalm 10:1-11

take the challenge

Do you ever wonder where God is when people you know about are getting away with bad things?

CHECK IT OUT

Write out David's urgent question in verse 1: "_____ _____ _____?"

When he sees all the horrible things evil people do and how they seem to get away with them, he says to himself (v. 11), "_____ _____ _____" and doesn't even look at what they are doing!" He thinks that God is not there for him, and that He is favoring the wicked, wealthy people over him.

make YOUR choice

Am I jealous of others because of what they have or the clothes they wear? _____ If yes, I can change my thinking...by being thankf

What are two things I can be thankful for today?_____

22

friday Psalm 10:12-18

take the challenge

Have you ever felt like your prayers were just bouncing off the ceiling? That God doesn't really hear you?

CHECK IT OUT

What does David say about the LORD in verse 17?

_____

_____

If you know Jesus as your Savior, He loves to listen to you and hear you talk to Him in prayer. What are some things we can bring to God in prayer? (Circle them and fill in the blanks.)   Hurts - dreamss - desiress - struggles - needs - _____ - _____

make YOUR choice

Take time right now to fill in some of your prayer pages in the front of this diary. Now pray for the people you have written down, and for yourself! Remember, God loves to l __ __ __ __ __ to my prayers!

saturday Psalm 11:1-7

take the challenge

What four-word sentence is on almost every American coin? Is it the truth?

CHECK IT OUT

How can you tell the psalmist is running from his enemies when he writes this psalm or prayer song to God? _____

_____

What were "the wicked" shooting at him? _____

What two things does he tell us God IS in verse 7?

_____ and _____

make YOUR choice

Circle some things that I need to trust God for: good friends - help with a test at school - moving to a new town or school - the courage to do what's right - boldness to tell others about Jesus -

_____ (List one of your own!)

3

Do you ask God questions? Do you request help from God? The psalmist does...

Circle the numbers of the Psalms that start with a question. Put a star beside the ones that start with a request for help.

12   13   14
15   16   17

SUNDAY Psalm 12:1-8

take the challenge

Do you have the right to say anything you please?

CHECK IT OUT

List three wrong ways of talking from verses 2 & 3.

_____, _____, _____

Where can you find pure and perfect words (v. 6)?

_____

make YOUR choice

What have I bragged about, lied about, exaggerated about, or flattered someone about in the last week? _____

_____

Lord, I want to have _____ lips today. Help me say wise and kind and true things.

24

MONDAY Psalm 13:1-6

take the challenge

There are times in everyone's life when it's hard to see God!

CHECK IT OUT

How was the writer feeling (v.2)?_____

_____ What did he think God

was doing (v.1)?_____

List three actions he took when he remembered God's

goodness (vv. 5-6). T_____

R_____ S_____

make YOUR choice

The next time I feel sad or lonely, I will think of God's goodness and

t_____, r_____

and s_____.

TUESDAY Psalm 14:1-7

take the challenge

The word "fool" means "empty-headed".

CHECK IT OUT

How does God describe the fool? Verse 1-He says:

"_____."

Verses 1 & 3 - His actions are: _____

_____

Verse 5 - He feels: _____

_____

make YOUR choice

How have I been foolish in the past? _____

_____

I don't want to be a fool! I will do my best to _____

God (v. 2).

25

WEDNESDAY Psalm 15:1-5

take the challenge

Wouldn't you like to be at home in God's presence?

CHECK IT OUT

This describes a man who dwells with God:

His walk is righteous or blameless. **(T or F)**

His speech is truthful. **(T or F)**

He treats his neighbor badly. **(T or F)**

He honors those who sin. **(T or F)**

He accepts bribes. **(T or F)**

make YOUR choice

I want to do what it takes to be at home (comfortable) with God! (Put a star by any of the things listed above that I may need to change to be closer to my Heavenly Father.)

thursday Psalm 16:1-11

take the challenge

So what is it like in the presence of God?

CHECK IT OUT

Write the verse number from this Psalm that tells us each of the benefits (following list) of being in God's presence. (Put the verse number in the box provided.)

Safety: [ ]   **Instruction:** [ ]

Gladness/Rejoicing: [ ]   **and** [ ]

Pleasure: [ ]

make YOUR choice

God is always with me! What can I do to help myself remember that?

_____

_____

friday Psalm 17:1-7

 take the challenge

How's your heart?

CHECK IT OUT

Who is the writer talking to?_____

So who is testing or checking his heart (v. 3)?_____

_____What did He find?

_____ In other words, his

heart was pure and open and honest before God!

make YOUR choice

What does God know about me that I wouldn't want to tell anyone

else? _____ God,

help me talk to You like the psalmist did. I don't want to hide anything

from You!

saturday Psalm 17:8-15

 take the challenge

What do you do when you think something is going to hit your eye?

CHECK IT OUT

How fragile and important our eyes are!

Complete this phrase from verse 8: "Keep me as the

_____ _____ _____

_____" God hides us from whom? (v 9)

make YOUR choice

_____

Thank you, God, that You consider me so precious, and that You are

committed to protecting me!

Chart Your Course

4

Look for these words as you read this week!

Buckler = Shield

Horn = A symbol of strength

Avenge = To get even with someone

Firmament = Skies

Banners = Flags

SUNDAY Psalm 18:1-12

take the challenge

What are some things that you need to be strong to be able to do?

CHECK IT OUT

List five words from verse 2 that give us pictures of God's strength:

Knowing God's great strength, what did the psalmist do when he felt "distressed" (v. 6)? _____.

make YOUR choice

When I feel weak or helpless, what should I do (like David did)?

_____

_____

MONDAY Psalm 18:13-24

take the challenge

Do you ever feel overwhelmed, like you are drowning because you are too busy… or lonely… or your work is too hard?

CHECK IT OUT

Which verse in today's passage tells how God will rescue you from "drowning" in your difficulties? [ ]

Verse 19 tells us why God chooses to rescue or deliver you: "because He _____ _____ _____." WOW! That's pretty awesome, isn't it?

make YOUR choice

I am (circle any that are true): a nobody to God - just another number to God - a somebody that God delights in - unnoticed by God - loved by God - rescued by God

TUESDAY Psalm 18:25-36

take the challenge

What makes a person great?

CHECK IT OUT

Who arms you with strength? _____

Who makes your way perfect? _____

What does God do to make you great (v. 35)?

_____

make YOUR choice

How can I become a great person? (Check the correct statement.)

[ ] Get good grades   [ ] Draw attention to myself with fancy clothes

[ ] Boss my friends around and show them who's in charge

[ ] Trust God and wait for Him

29

WEDNESDAY Psalm 18:37-50

take the challenge

Do you ever feel like "getting even" with someone who treats you unfairly?

CHECK IT OUT

Write down words from today's passage that refer to David's "enemies"? _____

_____   _____

Who won these battles against his enemies? _____

Write out the words of praise in verse 46 that David shouted out in his celebration of victory? "_____

_____

_____"

make YOUR choice

This week, I will (check one): ___ Try to get back at those who hurt me.
___ Let God take care of those who hurt me.

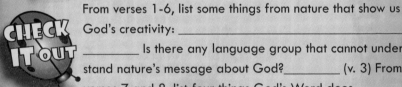

thursday Psalm 19:1-14

take the challenge

Wouldn't it be great if everything we saw reminded us of our Creator?

CHECK IT OUT

From verses 1-6, list some things from nature that show us God's creativity: _____

_____ Is there any language group that cannot understand nature's message about God? _____ (v. 3) From verses 7 and 8, list four things God's Word does.

_____

_____

_____

_____

make YOUR choice

I want to learn more about God by:
_____ Paying close attention to His creation.
_____ Reading and studying His Word.

friday Psalm 20:1-9

take the challenge

Who do you trust to meet your needs?

CHECK IT OUT

Verse 7 lists two things that some people trust in:

_____ and

_____

Pick out of the word puzzle (circle them) some things that people nowadays wrongly trust instead of God.

```
A S O F R I E N D S Y J A
L T H O M E A Y N K B O L
Y N O O D A S R I T E B K
E E O P U L M R I C A S P
N R O X L P A R E T U S S
O A O N Y A E U I U T S H
M P O P U L A R I T Y S L
```

make YOUR choice

Lord, help me rely on _____ to care for me and meet my needs.

saturday Psalm 21:1-13

take the challenge

What will your life be like if you rely upon God?

CHECK IT OUT

Match the verse numbers below to the good things that come from relying on God's strength.

_____ Joyful/Happy/Rejoicing   **A – verse 4**

_____ Receives the desire of his heart   **B – verse 2a**

_____ Receives what he asks for   **C – verse 13**

_____ Lives a long life   **D – verse 2b**

_____ Blessed with eternal blessings   **E – verse 1**

_____ The Lord is exalted   **F – verse 6**

make YOUR choice

What do I need to rely on God's strength for this week?

_____

_____

wk.

WEEKLY PASSAGES COVERED
Psalms 22:1-25:22

5

Psalm 22 - Psalm of the Suffering Savior

Psalm 24 - Psalm of the Mighty King

Chart Your Course

Psalm 23 - Psalm of the Kind Shepherd

Psalm 2 - Psalm of the Forgiving Teacher

SUNDAY Psalm 22:1-11

take the challenge

These are the words of Jesus, recorded hundreds of years before He spoke them!!

CHECK IT OUT

Copy the first question in verse one "_____ _____, _____ _____, _____ _____ _____ _____ _____?"

Look up Mark 15:34, and copy the words Jesus said on the cross: "_____ _____, _____ _____, _____ _____ _____ _____ _____?"

make YOUR choice

God loved me so much that He _____ His own Son in order to save me from my sin.

MONDAY Psalm 22:12-21

These words paint a picture of Jesus' experience on the cross hundreds of years before it happened!

Match the phrase from Psalm 22 with the correct New Testament passage:

_____ "They look and stare upon me"

_____ "My tongue sticks to the roof of my mouth"

_____ "They have pierced my hands and feet"

_____ "They divide my garments among them"

A - John 19:23

B - John 20:25-27

C - Luke 23:35

D - John 19:28

I can trust every word in the Bible, because what each verse says is

always _____.

TUESDAY Psalm 22:22-31

How can we possibly praise, worship, and rejoice after reading this picture of Christ's suffering?

The answer is here!

Verse 24 - God _____ the cry of His Son!

Verse 26 - Because of this, our heart will _____

_____.

Verse 27 - Who will turn to the Lord? _____

_____

How many times can you count the words "praise or "worship" in this passage? ☐

I can praise the Lord for Christ's suffering because He _____ me! Who can I share this Good News with today? _____

33

WEDNESDAY Psalm 23:1-6

take the challenge

Let's read the most well known Psalm in the world!

CHECK IT OUT

What does the Shepherd do? (Fill in the verse number for each action.) Leads ☐ Comforts ☐

Provides rest ☐ Provides water ☐

Provides food ☐ Protects ☐

Who is the shepherd? _____ (See

make YOUR choice

also John 10:11.) Who are the sheep?_____

Because Jesus my Shepherd loves me, I will f_____ Him.

---

thursday Psalm 24:1-10

take the challenge

Can a gentle shepherd also be a mighty king?

CHECK IT OUT

What are the four requirements for a person to get close to God (v. 4)?

1. _____ hands

2. _____ heart

3. Not lifted his soul to _____

4. Doesn't swear by what is false or untrue

make YOUR choice

What in my heart or life is keeping me from being really close to God?

_____

_____ God, cleanse me so that

I can come close to You, the King of Glory!

 **friday** Psalm 25:1-11

 take the challenge

Who is your favorite teacher ever?

CHECK IT OUT

As you read these verses, count how many times you find any word that means teach or guide, and write that number here _____. How is this teacher described in verses 5 and 8? _____

_____

make YOUR choice

I want to learn from the best Teacher! What can I do every day to learn from Him? _____

_____

---

saturday Psalm 25:12-22

take the challenge

Which is more important: how you feel or what you know?

CHECK IT OUT

Circle the words from verses 16-19 that describe how David felt **happy, confident, friendly, proud, lonely, hated, troubled, distressed, loved**

What did David know that God would do for Him?

Verse 12 _____

Verse 14 _____

Verse 20 _____

 make YOUR choice

Verse 21 _____

Sometimes I may *feel* _____. But I *know* that God _____. I need to be basing my choices on the truth I know about God, not my untrustworthy feelings.

35

6

Chart Your Course

DO YOU KNOW WHERE YOU ARE?

In Ephesians, Paul wants to assure believers that they are "In Christ" - secure in Him! How many times in Chapter 1 can you find the phrases "In Christ," "In Him," or "In Whom"?_____
As a believer, I live in Christ (1:1-2:6) and He lives in me (2:22)!

SUNDAY Ephesians 1:1-6

take the challenge

Have you ever waited to see if you will be chosen for a team, a part in a play, or to do a special job?

CHECK IT OUT

Read Ephesians 1:1-6 to find out:

WHO has chosen you?_____

WHEN were you chosen?_____

WHAT have you been chosen for?_____

make YOUR choice

Knowing that Christ has chosen me to be His child should make me want to _____
_____.

MONDAY Ephesians 1:7-14

take the challenge

Learn a new Bible word! Redemption means "being purchased and set free by paying a price."

CHECK IT OUT

In what two verses do you see the word redemption? ⬡ and ⬡. We have redemption through

what? Through _____ _____.

This is the price Jesus paid to set us free or forgive

make your choice

us from what? Our _____.

Christ purchased me! Since I am His possession (v. 14), what can I do to serve Him today? _____

TUESDAY Ephesians 1:15-23

take the challenge

Have you ever been faced with something that you thought was too hard for you?

CHECK IT OUT

Paul prayed for the believers that they would know the

greatness of the power of God. In verses 19-20 of this

passage, we read that the power that is available to

us who believe is the same power that R_____

H_____ F_____ the D_____!

make your choice

Since Christ's resurrection power is available to me, what can I do today that I thought was too hard for me? _____

_____

37

WEDNESDAY Ephesians 2:1-7

take the challenge

Do you ever get to thinking that you are a pretty good person, better than a lot of other people you see?

CHECK IT OUT

What does God say you were like before Jesus saved you (vv. 1-3)? _____

_____

_____

make YOUR choice

Since God looked at my sinful life through the eyes of mercy and love (v. 4), can I see others through His eyes? What sinner (like me!) can I show God's love and mercy to today? _____

_____

thursday Ephesians 2:8-13

take the challenge

Do you ever feel like bragging because of how good you are or how hard you work for God?

CHECK IT OUT

Unscramble these three words from verse 8.

ercag _____ tihaf_____

ftig _____ *THAT'S SALVATION!* And in verse 10:

ormpkwhanis _____

It's all about God's work, not mine!

make YOUR choice

I choose to (circle one):   **Be God's workmanship**

                            Do things my own way

friday Ephesians 2:14-18

 take the challenge

Our world is full of conflict: conflict between nations, conflict between political parties, conflict in families. But what about peace?

CHECK IT OUT

Who is our peace? _____ Reconcile means "join together or bring back together." What does God use to reconcile man to Himself (v.16)?

_____

GOD

When each of us draws closer to God, we also get closer to each other!

make YOUR choice

Who am I trusting to bring peace to the world and to my life? The President? Our military? My pastor or teacher? My parents? _____

Whom should I look to for peace? _____

saturday Ephesians 2:19-22

 take the challenge

Now that God has reconciled us to Himself and each other, what are we joined together to become?

CHECK IT OUT

What is God building as He joins us together?

_____

_____

_____

 make YOUR choice

As a part of God's Holy Temple (or dwelling place), I want to be

_____.

God's presence in my life makes me_____

_____. 39

7

Chart Your Course

Do you love a good MYSTERY?

In the Bible, the word **MYSTERY** means a truth that was hidden by God in the past but is now revealed to those in His family. Read His Word every day this week to find a special secret just for you, God's child!

SUNDAY Ephesians 3:1-7

take the challenge

Have you heard the Jewish people called "God's Chosen People"?

CHECK IT OUT

The word "heir" means "someone who has inherited something." In verse 6, this inheritance is the promise of Christ. Who can share in the promise of Christ?

Both Jews and _____.

(A "Gentile" is anyone who is not of Jewish descent.)

make YOUR choice

Today's MYSTERY is that anyone who believes in the promise of Christ can be one of "God's chosen people." That includes me! Have I believed the promise of Christ?
Yes / No

MONDAY Ephesians 3:8-13

take the challenge Do you ever feel unimportant or ignored?

CHECK IT OUT What did Paul (the writer of Ephesians) call himself? (Circle one.) **The greatest / The least of all God's saints (people)** In spite of how unimportant Paul felt, God had a great task (job) to accomplish through him (v. 8). What was this task? To p_____ to (or among) the _____.

make YOUR choice Verse 12 says that because of Christ, we have access to God (in prayer). Pray right now and ask God to use you for His eternal purpose: *Dear Lord, work in my heart and life and help me to make an eternal difference in this world where I live. Thank you for saving me and giving me Your Spirit Use me for Your glory!*

TUESDAY Ephesians 3:14-21

take the challenge Close your eyes and think of what wonderful things God can do in your life!

CHECK IT OUT What did Paul pray for his friends? For money? **Yes / No** For fame? **Yes / No** For good grades? **Yes / No** For strength and power? **Yes / No**

He also prayed that they would know what (v. 19)? _____ No matter what you ask for, God can do more!

make YOUR choice What did I think of with my eyes closed?_____

_____

Do I trust God to do even more marvelous things than that in my life? **Yes / No**

41

WEDNESDAY Ephesians 4:1-7

take the challenge

Do you want to live the way Christ called you to live?

CHECK IT OUT

God gives believers a "job description" in this passage. (Check the ones that describe Jesus.)

- [ ] **Lowliness means to be humble.**
- [ ] **Meekness means to be gentle.**
- [ ] **Longsuffering and forbearing means to be patient.**

make YOUR choice

The next time I am impatient or tired of waiting for someone, I will

_____.

The next time someone slows me down because they need help, I will

_____

thursday Ephesians 4:11-16

take the challenge

Did you know that your pastor and your teachers are special gifts of God to the church?

CHECK IT OUT

The "body of Christ" is the church. God wants His church (that's us!) to grow to be as strong and effective as it can possibly be. List some of the people He gives us to help us grow:

_____

_____.

make YOUR choice

What do I say to someone when they give me a gift? Have I ever thanked God for my pastor or teachers? _____ Could I write a little encouragement card to one of them today to let them know how much I appreciate them? I will write a note or card to: _____ I will think about what God may want me to do to prepare to serve as a gift to His church.

friday Ephesians 4:17-24

take the challenge
Is your life different from others who don't believe in Christ? God says there should be a difference between the old self and the new self.

CHECK IT OUT
V. 17- "Gentiles" here refers to unbelievers. Are we to live like unbelievers? _____ Verse 22- What are we to do with our old way of life ("former conversation")? _____ _____ Verse 23 says we are to think differently! Verse 24 tells us how our new self is created. How? _____

make YOUR choice
Sign your name under the sentence below that you would like to say to God:
1) *Lord, I want You to help me "put off" or get rid of the old part of me that displeases You. Amen.* _____
2) *Lord, I'm not ready to give up some of my old thoughts and habits, even if they aren't pleasing to You. Amen.* _____

saturday Ephesians 4:25-32

take the challenge
Do you really want to know some of the things God wants you to get rid of?

CHECK IT OUT
God lists several sins here, and also what we are to replace those sins with. Verse 25: Instead of lying, speak _____ _____. Verse 26: Don't stay _____ _____ all night. Verse 28: Instead of stealing, _____ so that you can give to the needy. Verse 29: "Corrupt communication" means trash talk, bad language, or unkind words. Verses 31 and 32: Instead of being bitter and angry, we are to be _____ and forgive.

make YOUR choice
I am asking God to help me replace this sin:_____
_____ with this new attitude or action:

_____ 43

8

WHO DO YOU IMITATE?
**A movie star? A sports hero?
A favorite teacher?**

HOW DO YOU IMITATE THIS PERSON?
**Dress like them? Talk like them?
Eat the same foods?**

WHY DO YOU IMITATE THEM?
**Because you admire or look up
to them and wish you could be like them.**

God WANTS us to imitate His Son!

chart your course

SUNDAY Ephesians 5:1-7

take the challenge

IMITATE HIS LOVE

CHECK IT OUT

How did Christ show His love for us? _____

_____ If Christ gave

Himself up for us, we should be able to "give up" our

selfish sins to fellowship with Him. List some of these

sins found in verses 3-5: _____

_____

_____

make your choice

I choose to imitate Christ's love by giving up this sin:

_____.

MONDAY Ephesians 5:8-14

IMITATE HIS LIGHT

Light helps us see things clearly. As you read today's passage, count how many times you see the word light.

Darkness hides shameful sins (vv. 11-12) but the light of Christ's righteousness exposes sin so that we can get rid of it and God will be pleased.

Check one:

☐ I want to hide my sin so no one will know about it.

☐ I want Christ's light (in the Bible) to show me my sin so that I can get rid of it and please God.

TUESDAY Ephesians 5:15-21

IMITATE HIS WISDOM

God wants us to be wise and alert in using our time. What does He want us to understand (v. 17)?

_____

_____

What could keep us from being alert and wise (v.18)?

_____

Some ways I waste time are:_____

_____ I can use my time wisely

for God today by: _____

_____

45

WEDNESDAY Ephesians 5:22-33

take the challenge

IMITATE HIM IN YOUR HOME

CHECK IT OUT

Here we see God's perfect pattern for the church and the home!

A. Christ *loves* the _____.

Husband *loves* his _____.

B. Church *submits* to _____.

Wife *submits* to _____.

Which of these words means the same thing as submit?
(Use your dictionary!) **REBEL   OBEY   YIELD   RESIST**

make YOUR choice

What are some TV shows I've watched recently? _____
_____

Which ones follow God's pattern for the family? _____
_____

Which ones do not? _____

thursday Ephesians 6:1-9

take the challenge

IMITATE HIS OBEDIENCE

CHECK IT OUT

In today's scripture, two groups of people
are commanded to obey someone. Who are they?

Verse 1 _____ obey _____

Verse 5 _____ obey _____

Verses 6-7 tell us that this obedience is not for the sake of

people, but for whom? _____

make YOUR choice

Keep track of how many times today you obey your parents
immediately, cheerfully, and without arguing. [ ]
Remember, you are doing it for God!

friday — Ephesians 6:10-17

take the challenge

IMITATE HIS WARFARE

CHECK IT OUT

This passage describes a Christian warrior. Who is the enemy?
_____ List the pieces of
spiritual armor: (v. 14a) _____
(v. 14b) _____ (v. 15) _____
(v. 16) _____ (v. 17a) _____
(v. 17b) _____ and always (v. 18) _____
_____.

Who provides the power and the armor to defeat the enemy?
_____

make YOUR choice

How am I preparing for spiritual warfare each day?
_____
_____

saturday — Ephesians 6:18-24

take the challenge

IMITATE HIM BY PRAYER AND CONCERN FOR OTHERS

CHECK IT OUT

According to these verses:
WHEN are we to pray?_____
_____
WHO are we to pray for?_____
_____
WHAT are we to pray about?_____
_____

make YOUR choice

Make a promise and set a time to pray every day! I will pray for others
every day at _____
(Fill in time of day, then
use this chart to keep
track of how well you
keep your promise!)

	M	T	W	TH	F	S	SUN
WK 1							
WK 2							

47

9

The Book of Esther – one of only two Biblical books named after a woman – moves like a dramatic play! Take a look at some of the characters and the setting...

ESTHER – her Persian name meant star, and she became a "star" in the history of the Jews. **HADASSAH** - Esther's Jewish name which meant "flower". She was a Jewish orphan taken captive to Babylon. **MORDECAI** – Esther's Jewish uncle who raised her. **XERXES** (famous Greek title for his Persian name, **AHASUERUS**) – King of Persia from 486 – 465 BC. **HAMAN** – the king's cruel official who wanted to kill all Jews, much like Hitler of the 1940's or Saddam Hussein and Osama Bin Laden today. **PERSIA** – an empire which spread from India to Egypt and whose capitol was Babylon. This is now modern-day **IRAQ**!

SUNDAY Esther 1:1-12

take the challenge

Have you ever been invited to a really fancy banquet or maybe a wedding reception . . . that lasted SEVEN DAYS??

CHECK IT OUT

Persian King Xerxes (Ahasuerus) gave a big _____ for all the _____ of his kingdom. It was in the royal winter place of Shushan (Susa). Name three things you would have seen there:

_____ _____ _____ Whom did the king want to bring in to show off her beauty? Queen _____

Can you number his seven assistants' names in alphabetical order?

___ **Mehuman**   ___ **Biztha**   ___ **Harbona**   ___ **Bigtha**

___ **Abagtha**   ___ **Zethar**   ___ **Carcas**

make YOUR choice

What do I notice about verses 7 and 10 that is **NOT** a good thing? _____

What choice will I make about drinking beer, wine, and other alcoholic drinks? _____

MONDAY Esther 1:13-22

take the challenge

Have any of your friends ever been really angry with you because you didn't come to their party?

CHECK IT OUT

Yesterday we read about King Xerxes inviting Queen Vashti to his special banquet party. Do you remember what she did? (Look at verse 17 and back at verse 12.) _____

• The king was upset by his wife's disobedience, so he called in his _____ (#) closest advisors. Circle the advisor who gave the best advice: **Carshena, Admatha, Tarshish, Shethar, Memucan, Marsena, Meres**

• Circle what the king decided to do: **Banish Queen Vashti & choose another / Send out a decree to all the people of the land that husbands are to be obeyed / Give all the ladies raises & special gifts**

make YOUR choice

Even though this was a heathen, godless culture of people, there is one important truth to see here: **God's plan for men is that they should be the (circle one) leaders / followers in the home. God's plan for women is that they should be the (circle one) leaders / followers in the home. I will decide right now to be God's kind of woman/ man someday when I have my own family.**

TUESDAY Esther 2:1-11

take the challenge

What do you think makes a girl truly beautiful?

CHECK IT OUT

What an exciting passage about the king's beauty contest! _____ was no longer the queen. Officers all over the land (does this remind you of Cinderella or what!) were to find _____ and bring them to the palace. H_____ was the one the king put in charge of all the _____ and their beauty treatments. _____ was a Jewish man who had been taken captive. He had raised his young orphaned niece, H_____. She was known as _____, and was so _____ that she got special attention.

make YOUR choice

Is there a person in my life who is trying to help me be a better Christian — a more "beautiful person"? Yes/ No Write that name here and let that person know how grateful you are for such loving care:

_____

49

WEDNESDAY Esther 2:15 - 23

take the challenge

Did you ever have to keep a special secret that you were not allowed to tell anyone until a certain time?

CHECK IT OUT

A LOT of action happens in today's story. Number the events in order according to when they occurred in the passage. [ ] The two would-be assassins were given the death penalty and hung. [ ] The king was more attracted to Esther than any other gal.

[ ] Bigthana and Teresh conspired against the king to assassinate (murder) him.

[ ] The king hosted a special Esther Banquet (feast) for all his top officials and made it a holiday. [ ] Esther was taken to see King Xerxes (Ahasuerus) at the winter palace.

[ ] Mordecai found out about the assassination plot and told Esther, who in turn told the king. [ ] The king put a royal crown on Esther's head, making her the new queen!

make YOUR choice

If I'm willing to make a difference in my world for Jesus, God WILL use me in ways I never imagined! Just like _____, I can be "salt" and "light" in my generation! (See Matthew 5:13.)

thursday Esther 3:8-15

take the challenge

Did you know that the persecution and planned annihilation (massacre) of the Jews (God's chosen people) did not begin with Hitler in World War II?

CHECK IT OUT

In the previous verses, a cruel man named H_____ (v. 8) had been promoted to "Vice President" of Persia. He hated Mordecai the Jew (E_____'s adoptive guardian) for never bowing to him or saluting him. He wanted Mordecai and all his people killed! In verse 9, he asks the king to write up a decree to _____ all the Jewish people living in Persia, and offers to help pay for this ethnic cleansing. Circle the officials of the land this decree was delivered to: **satraps - princes - nobles - jesters - lieutenants - governors - teachers**
This order included even the w_____ and c_____, and would begin and end on the _____ day.

make YOUR choice

Knowing that more of God's people are being persecuted or killed for their faith in our century than any other period of history — what can I do to help? (Circle one.) **Pray, Ignore this, Give to missions**

friday Esther 4:1-17

take the challenge

Have you ever been faced with the challenge to rescue someone else – maybe even a pet – from danger? Check out today's exciting account!

CHECK IT OUT

Put one of the following three names in front of the phrases describing what they did or said in today's verses: Mordecai - Esther - Hathach

_____ Mourned and wept in sackcloth and ashes.

_____ Ordered by Esther to find out what was wrong with her uncle.

_____ Urged Esther to go before the king and beg for his mercy on their people, the Jews.

_____ Asked Mordecai to have everyone pray and fast (go without eating) for her.

_____ Said, "If I perish, I perish!"

make YOUR choice

Someday I may be faced with a life-threatening situation where I will have to make a godly and courageous decision. How will I handle it?

_____

saturday Esther 5:1-14

take the challenge

Have you ever felt intimidated to talk to someone "important"?

CHECK IT OUT

Fill in the right words to complete the crossword puzzle below. On the (1 down) day, Esther faced the (2 down) on his (3 across). He held out his golden (4 down) to her, and offered her (5 across) his kingdom if she would tell him what was the matter. Esther asked him to have a (6 across) and invite evil (7 down). Haman let his wife, (8 down), and friends talk him into building a (9 down) on which to kill (10 across).

make YOUR choice

Remembering how brave Esther was, what hard thing will I attempt to do today with God's help? _____

_____

wvlc.

10

Have you noticed that God's name is not mentioned once in Esther? But yet God's "fingerprints" are seen all through it as He directs the amazing plot that saves His people from annihilation (all being killed).

Chart Your Course

Remember how Haman – the "Hitler" of his time – had a GALLOWS built to kill Mordecai the Jew? It was not a hanging gallows like this one you've probably see in old cowboy movies. It was a 75-foot high pole for killing a victim by impalement (stuck through the body like a spear), and then leaving the dead body hanging on the top for everyone to see.

SUNDAY   Esther 6:1-14

take the challenge

Has one of your teammates or classmates ever gotten an award, reward, or special recognition you thought you should have gotten?

CHECK IT OUT

Today we see another clue that God is working behind the scenes. Who do you think kept King Xerxes from being able to sleep?_____ When he read what he thought would be a boring Persian record book, who did he discover had saved his life from being assassinated? _____ Because this man had never been honored for his bravery, the king had _____ suggest to him what should be done. What did Haman suggest, thinking the king was referring to him (vv. 7-9)?_____
Who "got" to lead Mordecai the Jew through the streets, proclaiming his honor? _____ Afterwards, Haman ran to his _____, (circle one) laughing / crying / screaming.

make your choice

Who is always "behind the scenes" working in MY life for my good, even when I don't know it? _____

52

MONDAY Esther 7:1-7, 9-10

take the challenge

Have you ever heard the phrase, "Turn about's fair play"? Let's see what it means in today's episode!

CHECK IT OUT

Esther's private banquet with the _____ and _____ has begun. When the king asks for her petition (request) this time, she asks him to spare _____ life and that of her _____ from annihilation. When _____ is exposed for planning this whole evil plot, _____ suggests he be killed on the _____ he had made for _____. When did the furious king calm down? _____

make your choice

Just as Esther bravely shared her heart requests with the king, so I need to share **my** heart requests with the King of Kings in prayer. One important prayer request I have today is: _____

TUESDAY Esther 8:1-8, 11-13, and 15-17

take the challenge

Whom would you have liked to have been if you could go back in time? Mordecai, King Xerxes, Esther, or Haman

CHECK IT OUT

Look back at Esther 6:15 and 8:8. What do these verses tell us about a Persian king's decree? Since the Jewish massacre (mass murder) could not be reversed, the king, influenced by Queen _____, made and sent out another decree giving all the Jews in every province permission to _____ _____ (see v. 11) any and all forces that would attack them! _____ Esther's now rich and famous Uncle _____ had saved the Jewish race from total annihilation! Circle the things Mordecai was given: new shoes, **Haman's estate**, **Haman's royal ring**, 10 royal dogs, **blue and white royal robes**, silver gloves, **a large gold crown**, **a purple robe or coat**

make your choice

How did the Jews respond to the king's new decree in their behalf (v. 17)? _____ How should I respond to God's goodness in my life today? _____ 53

WEDNESDAY Esther 9:1-11, 16-17

take the challenge

Have you ever been bullied by someone? Mordecai had been bullied by proud Haman, but now he was great and Haman was dead!

CHECK IT OUT

Verse 4 tells us that Mordecai was now _____ in the king's palace. What four groups of government officials helped the Jews out because of their fear of Mordecai?

_____ _____ _____

_____ Can you unscramble some of the names of men killed by the Jews when they fought back?

THADAANSHARP _ _ _ _ _ _ _ _ _ _ _ _ _ _

LOPHAND _ _ _ _ _ _ _ _ _ _ _ _   **LADAIA** _ _ _ _ _ _ _ _

SARIAI _ _ _ _ _ _ _ _   **ROTHAPA** _ _ _ _ _ _ _

Altogether, the Jews killed _____ Persians on the _____ day of the month _____.

make YOUR choice

Look up James 4:10 in the New Testament. How can I be great like Mordecai became? _____

_____

thursday Esther 9:18-22, 28-10:3

take the challenge

Think about it! Since Jesus the Messiah was born from the Jewish race, what might have happened if Esther had not courageously saved the Jews from total annihilation?

CHECK IT OUT

The Jewish victory celebration – a _____ of _____ and _____ (v. 18) – developed into a yearly Jewish holiday or festival called _____ _____(vv.29-31). It is still celebrated in early spring each year. Mordecai became second only to the _____ and _____ among all the Jews because he always sought for (worked for) the _____ of his people and spoke up for their peace and welfare (10:3)!

make YOUR choice

Esther, a young lady with great courage, made a difference in the royal line of Jesus our Messiah. How can I make a difference in my world?

_____

_____

friday — Song of Solomon 2:1-13

take the challenge

Talk about time travel! Today we go back in time 500 years to the happy days of King Solomon . . . in love, no less!

CHECK IT OUT

King Solomon, the wisest man who ever lived, wrote a poem when he was younger about a Shulamite maiden he had fallen madly in love with. This long poem was called the _____ of _____. The young maiden was singing a love song to the man she loved. Write down three love terms she used to describe him here: 1. _____
2. _____ 3. _____

make YOUR choice

Someday I'll probably be in love with someone. I'd like the person of my dreams to be: (List three things.)

(1) _____
(2) _____
(3) _____

(Did you put "a Christian who loves the Lord" down as one of them??)

saturday — Song of Sol. 5:10 & 6:3

take the challenge

Do you ever think about what kind of person you will marry someday?

CHECK IT OUT

Match the following comparisons the maiden makes about her lover by drawing lines between them.

CHARACTERISTIC	BODY PART
Black as a raven	legs
Like beds of spice on balsam	head
Marble (alabaster) pillars	eyes
Purest fine gold	hair
Rods or bands of gold	mouth
Full of sweetness	cheeks
Drip with myrrh	lips
Like doves by the rivers and streams	hands/arms

make YOUR choice

She calls this young man not only her lover, but also her f_____.

Write out the first part of 6:3 here: "I am _____ _____." Can you say this about your relationship with the Lover of Your Soul, Jesus Christ? **Yes / No**

55

Titus 1:1-Philemon 25

11

Will you find any of these this week?

Pastors? False Prophets? Older women? Young men? Qualities of a Christian? How God saved us? Philemon? Onesimus?

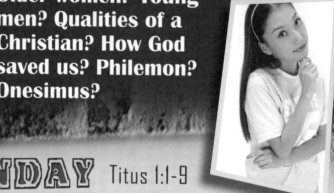

SUNDAY Titus 1:1-9

take the challenge

Can people in my church tell that I am a Christian who not only obeys God but also my parents?

CHECK IT OUT

Put a check mark next to the qualifications for someone who is a Pastor or elder? (vv. 6-9)

____ Blameless   ____ Not easily angered

____ Addicted to wine   ____ Husband of one wife

____ Holy   ____ Not greedy

____ Self controlled   ____Children who are unruly

____ Teaching whatever he wants

make your choice

Why do you think it would be important for a pastor to have children who are faithful Christians?_____

_____ What is one way people in my church can tell that I am an obedient Christian?_____

MONDAY Titus 1:10-16

take the challenge

What do you think a false prophet is?

CHECK IT OUT

Verse 16 says that, "They profess (or claim) to know God, but in works (or actions) they deny Him". What do you think John meant by this statement?

What are three sinful characteristics of Cretans?

(1)_____,

(2)_____,

(3)_____

make YOUR choice

Does this describe my life? **Yes / No**

Why or why not? _____

_____

TUESDAY Titus 2:1-10

take the challenge

Can you name some older men or women in your church that you look up to?

CHECK IT OUT

What are 3 characteristics of older "aged" women?

(1)_____,

(2)_____,

(3)_____

Those who watch godly young men should have nothing

_____ to say about them (v. 8). A bond slave or

servant should be "_____ to their masters".

make YOUR choice

Based on what I've have read, I think God wants me to act

_____.

WEDNESDAY Titus 2:11-15

take the challenge

What are 3 main qualities you think a good Christian should have?

CHECK IT OUT

List 3 ways verse 12 tells us to live.

1 _____ ,

2 _____ ,

3 _____

make YOUR choice

Which of these am I living out in MY Christian life?

Check those above and pray for help on any you can't check!

thursday Titus 3:4-15

take the challenge

Remember how you felt when you first asked Jesus to be your personal Savior? Were you excited? Did you tell anyone?

CHECK IT OUT

Circle the statements that describe how God saved us.

According to his mercy

Through our works of righteousness

Washing of

regeneration (rebirth)

Renewing of the Holy Spirit

By sending an angel to earth

Justified by his grace

make YOUR choice

Should I hang around with a foolish, argumentative person? (v. 11)

Yes / No Why or why not? _____

friday Philemon 1-7

take the challenge

Who is a person you like to write a letter or send e-mails to?

CHECK IT OUT

List the people Paul is writing to:

Paul heard about the _____

and _____ of Philemon's church (v.5).

make YOUR choice

How would I want people to describe me? _____

_____

_____

saturday Philemon 10-21

take the challenge

What should I do if I have wronged someone or taken something that is not mine?

CHECK IT OUT

Paul called Onesimus, the prisoner, his own

_____ in verse 10 and his dear or beloved

_____in verse 16. What did Paul say he

would do if Onesimus had wronged someone or

taken something (v. 19)? _____

_____

make YOUR choice

Is there someone I've wronged or something that I've taken that I

need to return **Yes / No** How will I make it right? _____

_____

59

12

Imagine what it would be like to be in jail alone, and to see Jesus.

The next thing you know, He's asking you to write a book. That's what's happening in the book of Revelation. Check it out for yourself!

SUNDAY Revelation 1:1-8

take the challenge

If someone said, "If you read this book you will be blessed (truly happy!)," would you read it?

CHECK IT OUT

Who wrote the book of Revelation, and who was the messenger? Writer: _____,

Messenger: _____ What will happen to those who read this book (v. 3)? They'll be " _____

_____ ". Who is this book written to (vv. 4-5)?

_____

_____

make YOUR choice

Why would it be important for me to read the book of Revelation?

_____

_____

MONDAY Revelation 1:9-16

Here is a lesson in the Greek alphabet: the first and last letters are Alpha and Omega.

Write the names of the seven churches to which John was writing.

1) _____
2) _____
3) _____
4) _____
5) _____
6) _____
7) _____

What did John see when he turned around (v. 13)?

Some words that I would use when describing Jesus to a friend are:

TUESDAY Revelation 1:17-20

How would you act in the presence of a King?

What did John do when he saw the angel?
_____

Circle the reason John did this (v. 17).

He was (circle one):

Joyful   **Afraid**   **Tired**

I can show respect when I worship God by _____

_____

61

WEDNESDAY Revelation 2:1-7

take the challenge

Have you ever had a close friend turn their back on you?

CHECK IT OUT

Circle the things that the church of Ephesus had done right (vv. 2-3):

Couldn't stand evil

Found false prophets　　　**Endured**

Sent out missionaries　　　**Had patience**

Many people were saved　　**Didn't give up**

make YOUR choice

What is one thing that I can do for Jesus today?

_____

_____

thursday Revelation 2:8-11

take the challenge

Is it difficult to live in poverty (having very little money)?

CHECK IT OUT

Jesus said He knew Smyrna's _____ and

_____, but yet they were r __ __ __ !

He told them in verse 10b to "be _____ unto

_____."

make YOUR choice

How would I react if I had to face death for what I believe?

_____

_____

_____

friday — Revelation 2:12-17

take the challenge

Are there people in your life that it is hard to live the Christian life around?

CHECK IT OUT

The Church of Pergamum (Pergamos) was listening to the false, ungodly teaching/doctrine of B_____ and the N_____. They needed to "R_____" (v. 16).

make YOUR choice

What is one way I can keep myself pure while living around sinful people? _____
_____

saturday — Revelation 2:18-29

take the challenge

Have you ever heard the statement, "it was as if his eyes could see right through me"?

CHECK IT OUT

What were five good things Jesus knew about this church of Thyatira (v. 19)? (1) _____, (2) _____, (3) _____, (4) _____, (5) _____

God said he would _____her on a bed (of suffering or sickness)! God tells them to _____ _____ to what they have until He comes.

make YOUR choice

Verse 23 says that Christ searches our minds and hearts. What is one area of sinful thinking that I need to change? _____
_____

13

Look for these
mysterious symbols as
you read this week:

**seven stars, brotherly
love, lightening,
lukewarm, seven seals,
crowns of gold, lion
of Judah,
the lamb**

Chart your course

SUNDAY Revelation 3:1-6

take the challenge

What do you think God will do
to churches that are "asleep"
instead of active for God?

CHECK IT OUT

What did John say the people should remember?
(Circle the correct answers.)

What they had received - To stay true

To repent - To remain holy

What they had heard - To keep His Word

make your choice

What should I do if I have done something wrong?

MONDAY Revelation 3:7-13

take the challenge

Did you know that Philadelphia means brotherly love?

CHECK IT OUT

What are three reasons (v. 8) why God could trust the Church of Philadelphia with an "open door" of opportunity? They had (1) _____,

(2) _____ and (3) _____.

make YOUR choice

Obedience shows that we love God. How am I keeping God's Word? _____

TUESDAY Revelation 3:14-22

take the challenge

Are there areas in my life where I try to take care of things myself or trust in my own ability?

CHECK IT OUT

Christ tells this church of Laodicea in verse 16,

that because they are _____, neither

_____ nor _____, he was going to

_____ them out of his _____!

make YOUR choice

In this passage lukewarm means not being 100 percent committed to Christ. What is one area in my life where I am being lukewarm? (Circle it.)

regular Bible reading   -   friendships   -   hard work
using my tongue wisely   -   obedience to parents
honesty   -   daily prayer

WEDNESDAY Revelation 4:1-11

John walks through the door into Heaven. Let's see what Heaven will be like.

Find the hidden words below that describe Heaven:

Jasper
Emerald
Crystal
Gold
Rainbow

R	E	P	S	A	J	E	J	L	B	U	Q	K	E
S	A	O	L	D	T	X	D	N	Y	R	Q	M	L
W	D	I	C	R	Y	S	T	A	L	B	E	I	R
O	T	L	N	C	C	H	E	T	W	R	O	S	S
X	X	E	Z	B	I	P	S	N	A	P	A	E	T
D	L	O	G	K	O	L	W	L	U	I	H	K	L
H	M	K	E	L	T	W	D	P	D	K	R	L	K

make YOUR choice

What did the four creatures say to the One Who sat on the throne? "You are _____ to receive _____."

What are some of the things for which I can praise and worship God? Who can I write a thank you letter to, thanking them for being one of God's servants? _____

thursday Revelation 5:1-7

take the challenge

Did you know that one of the names for Jesus is "the Lamb of God"?

CHECK IT OUT

Who was the One worthy to open the scroll and break the seals? The _____ of [that is from] the _____ of _____; the _____ of D_____; a L_____ (v. 6)

make YOUR choice

Write a sentence of praise to God for sending the Lamb of God to die for you and take away your sins.

friday  Revelation 5:8-14

 Did you know that there will be people from every tribe and nation that will live with God forever in Heaven?

 In the last part of verse nine, it says that people were redeemed by [purchased for] God out of what four groups? From every . . .

_____ _____ _____ _____

God wants people from all over the world to be His children.

 Are there children in my school or neighborhood that are not accepted because they are different (skin color or speak with an accent)? **Yes / No**
What are three things I could do to be friends with them? *Invite them to my Birthday Party - **Invite them to church** - Sit with them at lunch - Have them sleep overnight - **Share Jesus with them** - Introduce them to my friends - Play with them on the playground*

saturday Revelation 6:1-8

The horses you read about in Chapter 6 represent ruling forces that make things happen on the earth. So when you think of a horse in these verses think of rulers in the world and the ability they have been given by God.

Draw a line from the riders on the four horses to what they will do.

White horse	Bring famine, high food cost
Red horse	Conquer
Black horse	Remove peace; bring war
Pale (tan) horse	Death to one fourth of the world

The future time you read about today is a time of war and hardship. The Bible teaches that those who have trusted Christ will not have to go through this time, but will be taken to Heaven to be with God. Who could you share the gospel with today so they would not have to go through this time?

_____ .

Did You know?

The book of Revelation reveals what is going to happen soon in what we call "the Tribulation." "Tribulation" means a time of great worldwide suffering because of God's judgment on the sins of man. It is something no one would ever want to go through!

SUNDAY Revelation 6:9-17

take the challenge

Can you imagine an earthquake so bad that you wanted the rocks to fall on you and hide you?

CHECK IT OUT

After the fifth seal was opened, what did the people say who were under the altar? In verse 11 each of the souls was given a white robe, which represented eternal life. Describe in the box what you think the earthquake in verse 12 was like.

make YOUR choice

I will write a one-sentence prayer to God thanking him for my salvation, and that because of Him, I don't have to go through the tribulation: _____

_____

MONDAY Revelation 7:1-8

take the challenge

Why do you think God put a seal on the foreheads of the servants of God?

CHECK IT OUT

Unscramble the words to find the names of the 12 tribes of Judah. DAHJU _____ LPATIHNA _____

SSIARHAC _____ URENEB _____

NASSEMHA _____ LONZUBA or LUNZUBE

(different in different Bible translations) _____

DAG _____ MESINO _____ HPESJO _____

HARES _____ VEIL _____ JMANBINE _____

make YOUR choice

If I was one of these servants, how would I tell these people that had survived the earthquake about Christ?_____

_____ How can I share with someone this

week how I came to know Jesus? (This is my "testimony.")

_____

_____

TUESDAY Revelation 7: 9-17

take the challenge

Whom do you think the great multitude will be that is standing before the throne?

CHECK IT OUT

Who are these people that are wearing white

robes and worshipping God? (Circle one.)

(1) People who've been washed clean in Jesus'

blood (2) soldiers (3) unsaved people

The angels stood around God's_____ and

_____ Him.

make YOUR choice

How can I worship God with my words today? _____

_____

WEDNESDAY Revelation 8:1-13

take the challenge

What happened when the angel blew the trumpet?

CHECK IT OUT

The first trumpet - _____ and _____ mixed [mingled] with _____ The second trumpet - A huge, fiery _____ thrown into the _____ The third trumpet - A _____ _____ on fire fell on the _____ and _____ The fourth trumpet - A _____ part of the sun, moon, and stars turned _____

make YOUR choice

Because I know _____ as my personal _____, I won't have to be on _____ to go through these terrible events. Praise the Lord!

thursday Revelation 9:1-12

take the challenge

In this passage the fifth trumpet is sounded and we see the first "woe." What do you think the woe is?

CHECK IT OUT

What do you think the Abyss or the bottomless pit was?

_____

Why do you think the Lord allowed the locusts to torture the people for five months but not kill them? _____

_____

The locusts looked like _____ prepared for _____ according to verse 7.

make YOUR choice

Who do I know who is not a Christian and will have to go to Hell for their sins?_____ Will I tell them this week how to be saved? **Yes / No**

friday Revelation 9:13-21

 take the challenge
How do you think the people will respond after more suffering?

CHECK IT OUT
What was the job of the four angels who were bound at the river Euphrates (v. 15)? What three things did the horses breathe out of their mouths (v. 17)?

make YOUR choice
According to verse 21, did the people repent? **Yes / No**

How do I respond after I've been disciplined? (Circle one.) Pout - Get angry and yell - Cry - Say I'm sorry but don't mean it - Am truly sorry and make it right

Do I always respond (repent of my sin) the first time?

saturday Revelation 10:1-11

 take the challenge
In your reading today, notice the angel's focus on God's power in verses 5 and 6?

CHECK IT OUT
The angel in verse 9 tells John, the writer, to

"T_____ and e_____" the little scroll

or book of God. How did he say it tasted (v. 10)?

_____

make YOUR choice
How can I "take and eat" of God's Book, the Bible, daily?

_____
_____
_____

wk.
15

Chart Your Course

Look for some strange figures in this week's passages:

the two witnesses, the woman and the dragon, the beast out of the sea, and the beast out of the earth.

SUNDAY Revelation 11:1-12

take the challenge

God tells the two witnesses to prophesy for 1,260 days! "Prophesy" means to speak forth God's message.

CHECK IT OUT

What will happen to those who try to harm the two witnesses? _____

_____ After the two witnesses were killed and then brought back to life, how did God call them up to Heaven (v. 12)? "_____ _____

_____!" Who saw them go? _____ _____

make your choice

Am I being a witness to others of what God tells me from His Word?
Yes/No What is the one thing I can share with another person today?

_____

MONDAY Revelation 11:13-19

take the challenge

What do you think the seventh trumpet will reveal? Who are the 24 elders?

CHECK IT OUT

One of the most famous musical scores that has ever been written, "The Hallelujah Chorus" by Handel, was based on the powerful words of worship in verse 15. Write down the chorus the "great loud voices in Heaven" were singing on the music lines below.

make YOUR choice

Who do I know in Heaven? _____

How might that person be worshipping Christ right now?

TUESDAY Revelation 12:1-9

take the challenge

Try drawing a picture of the dragon described in today's verses.

CHECK IT OUT

Do you have an idea who the male child represents – the one the woman gave birth to in verse 5?

Verse 9 tells us the dragon was really the d_____ and S_____.

make YOUR choice

What can I do to keep from being deceived by Satan's lies?

_____

_____ 73

WEDNESDAY Revelation 12:10-17

take the challenge

Did you know that "time, times, and a half time" refers to three and a half years of the tribulation, before the second coming of Christ?

CHECK IT OUT

Find some of the things that the loud voice said and circle them.

You have overcome the world - They overcame him with power

By the word of their testimony - Now has come salvation

They did not love their lives - Rejoice you heavens!

Because the devil was happy

Because he knows he has a short time - Woe to the earth

make YOUR choice

Why do you think Satan tries to tempt us? What could I do if Satan does try to tempt me? (circle them) Run - Pray - Ask a friend for help Read my Bible - Tell a teacher - Go to church - Hide in my room Just like Satan tempts me, he also tempts Christian leaders. This week I'll pray for a godly leader or missionary I know. The person I'll pray for is

_____.

thursday Revelation 13:1-10

take the challenge

The beast that comes out of the sea represents the Antichrist or Satan in a human body.

CHECK IT OUT

In verses 3 and 4, the reason the people will worship the beast (Antichrist) and give him power is because he begins his career as a peacemaker. This satanic power blasphemed, or slandered, God in three areas, according to verse 6. What are they? (1) His _____ (2) His _____ (3) Those who dwell/live in _____

make YOUR choice

Are there people in my life that are more important to me than God? If so, what should I do to change that? Jesus should always have first place in my life.

friday Revelation 13:11-18

take the challenge

Did you know the word "counterfeit" means fake or false? Counterfeit money is fake money.

CHECK IT OUT

This beast is the counterfeit Holy Spirit. Verse 14 tells us that he ordered the people to set up an _____ to the beast (v. 15). The image or idol was given the ability or power to give _____ to the image, to_____, and cause everyone who didn't worship or bow down to him to be _____. He also forced everyone to take (receive) a _____ in their _____ or _____ in order to _____ or _____ anything.

make YOUR choice

How do I know I'm not a counterfeit Christian? _____
_____
_____

saturday Revelation 14:1-7

take the challenge

Imagine what it would be like to be singing to Jesus Christ with thousands of people.

CHECK IT OUT

How many people were standing on Mt. Zion with the Lamb? _____
What was it that John heard? _____
_____ And whom do you think they were singing to? _____
_____ Verse 4 tells us these were the ones who were following the _____ wherever He went.

make YOUR choice

One of my favorite worship or praise songs is: _____
_____ Sing it to God right now.

Circle some of the important numbers you've seen in this mysterious book of Revelation:

Chart Your Course

58   **3 1/2**   **220**

666   **144,000**

SUNDAY   Revelation 14:8-13

take the challenge

The angel announces that God is going to destroy Babylon (the empire and its false religion). This is the city the beast has set up for himself.

CHECK IT OUT

How will those who don't know Jesus as Savior be tormented after being judged for their sins (vv. 10b-11)?_____

_____

_____

make YOUR choice

Those that take the mark and worship the beast will spend eternity in Hell. Jot down three people that you can tell about Jesus. Have you put them on your daily prayer list so you will remember to pray for them every day?

_____   _____

_____

MONDAY Revelation 14:14-20

 **take the challenge**

The time to reap has come, for the harvest of the earth is ripe. Reap means to bring the harvest in because it is fully grown.

 CHECK IT OUT

Unscramble some of the words that the angel spoke in verses 18-20:

CISEKL_____ IPER_____

PSRWENISE_____

PEGRAS_____ AHRET_____

make YOUR choice

LUSECTSR_____

Sometimes it is difficult to accept punishment even when we know we've done wrong. Next time I am disciplined, I will_____

_____

TUESDAY Revelation 15:1-8

take the challenge

John sees a sea of glass mixed with fire.

CHECK IT OUT

Fill in the blanks to finish the angels' song in verses 3 & 4.

"Great and _____ are your _____ Lord God Almighty. _____ and _____are your ways, _____ of the _____. Who will not _____ you, O Lord and bring glory to your name? For you alone are _____. All nations will come and _____ before you, for your righteous acts are revealed (or made manifest)."

make YOUR choice

Are there some actions that I need to confess to the Lord that would not bring glory to his name? What are they? _____

_____

Right now I will pray and ask God to forgive me.   77

WEDNESDAY Revelation 16:1-12

take the challenge

What does it feel like to be waiting for a punishment you deserve?

CHECK IT OUT

Fill in the blanks for each bowl of judgment or punishment that the angels poured out and what the result is:

Verse #	Bowl/Vial Judgment	Where poured	What punishment it caused
v. 2	First		
v. 3	Second		
v. 4	Third		
v. 8	Fourth		
v. 10	Fifth		
v. 12	Sixth		

make YOUR choice

God's judgments are always fair. Have I ever judged someone unfairly? **Yes / No** What can I do to make it right? _____

_____

thursday Revelation 16:13-21

take the challenge

The seventh bowl judgment includes a great earthquake and 100-pound hail stones. Have you ever been hit by a hailstone?

CHECK IT OUT

The earthquake was so big that the city split into _____ parts (v. 19). What was the name of the city where the kings gathered? _____

(This is the place where the nations of the world will gather for the great battle of Armageddon.) What did the people do as a result of the plague of hail (v. 21)?

_____

make YOUR choice

Because of man's sinfulness, war is sometimes used to settle disagreements. How do you think God would want people to settle disputes? I settle problems in my life by: _____

_____

friday Revelation 17:1-8

take the challenge

Today you will read about a very wicked woman (harlot or prostitute) who represents the worldwide religion of the end times.

CHECK IT OUT

Check the box that best describes the harlot (wicked end-time religion).

Verse 2a ☐ kings and rulers were involved ☐ only common people were involved

Verse 4a ☐ the religion was poor ☐ the religion was rich

Verse 4b ☐ the religion encouraged only a little sin ☐ the religion encouraged people to be very sinful

Verse 6 ☐ Christians (saints) were treated well ☐ Christians were martyred (killed)

Verse 6 makes it clear that in the end times if you have become a Christian and are not a part of this worldwide religion, your life will always be in danger. Many will be killed because they follow Jesus and take a stand against the sinfulness in the world.

make YOUR choice

Describe a situation in which I may have to take a stand for Jesus.

_____

Will I make a decision that when that time comes I will stand for Jesus?

☐ Yes ☐ No

---

saturday Revelation 17:9-18

take the challenge

Have you ever been in a situation that seemed like you had no chance to win? In the passage today, all the world powers turn to make war with Jesus. Who do you think will win?

CHECK IT OUT

What do the kings of the earth do to the Lamb in verses 12-14a? _____ _____ against Him. What will the Lamb (Jesus) do to them in verse 14b? He will _____ them! Why will He overcome them (v. 14b)? Because He is _____ of _____ and _____ of _____.

make YOUR choice

The next time you get into a situation that seems you have no way out, what should you do? Check the boxes that you think would please God. ☐ Pray for God's help.

☐ Talk to my parents about the problem. ☐ Scream at the top of my lungs.

☐ Tell God how great He is. ☐ Remember God is in control and trust Him.

☐ Start to cry. ☐ Give up. ☐ Talk to a spiritual leader in my church. 79

WEEKLY PASSAGES COVERED
Revelation 18:1-20:6

Queen of Babylon,
The White Horse,
The Dragon, A Mighty
Angel, Four Living Creatures,
The Lamb, and The Beast.

Which of these unique creatures would you like to run into? Find out which are good and which are evil this week. revealed to those in His family. Read His Word every day this week to find a special secret just for you, God's child!

SUNDAY   Revelation 18:1-8

take the challenge

Have you ever gotten involved with someone who is doing something bad? What did you do?

CHECK IT OUT

And the merchants of the earth grew (waxed, became) _____. Then in verses 4-8 John heard another voice shouting for separation. It cried: "_____ _____ of her." God wanted the Jewish nation to be separate from the worldly ways and sins of (circle one): **Jerusalem   Babylon   Sidon**

make YOUR choice

What are some things I really want to get that could result in my doing wrong? _____
_____
_____

MONDAY Revelation 18:9-19

take the challenge

Have you ever lost or had stolen, something that meant a lot to you?

CHECK IT OUT

The merchants of the world will weep when they see the great trade city of Babylon destroyed. They will mourn (weep) the city's downfall because they won't be able to carry on the business of the city and make lots of money. Pick the cargoes they'll mourn over in verses 12 and 13. Circle them (at least nine) in the word puzzle. All these things show us how rich in resources Babylon was.

B	E	A	S	T	S	P	E	E	H	S
G	O	L	D	D	S	E	D	N	Y	I
W	I	R	O	N	A	A	T	S	L	L
O	L	L	T	C	R	R	T	S	W	V
S	Y	M	A	R	B	L	E	E	O	E
E	R	O	E	K	I	S	W	V	O	R
S	O	K	H	R	T	W	D	A	D	E
R	V	E	W	B	R	U	O	L	F	N
O	I	N	T	M	E	N	T	S	A	I
H	C	I	N	N	A	M	O	N	A	W

make YOUR choice

Like these men, do you ever let money or things make you happy? **Yes/No** Why is it better to enjoy serving God than to enjoy having lots of money? _____
_____

TUESDAY Revelation 18:20-24

take the challenge

Have you ever been glad when someone who was hurting you and others finally got caught and punished?

CHECK IT OUT

In verse 22, what four kinds of musicians will never be heard from again? _____,
_____, _____ and
_____ The voice of the
b_____ and b_____ will
never be heard again either (v. 23).

make YOUR choice

The reason for the harsh judgment of the city of Babylon was because she led all the nations astray from God and she was guilty of murdering prophets and saints. How can I pray about those who have been misleading others? _____

WEDNESDAY Revelation 19:1-8

take the challenge

How many times do you see the worship word "Alleluia" or "Hallelujah" in today's verses? Write the number here: _____

CHECK IT OUT

Write a worship song of the great multitude from verse one on the megaphone below:

_____

_____

_____

make YOUR choice

Where, when, and how do I worship God? _____

_____

_____

thursday Revelation 19:9-16

take the challenge

Have you ever gone horseback riding?

CHECK IT OUT

The white horse is a symbol of Christ's triumph over the forces of wickedness and His return to earth in glory. This is the same way a king would return from battle. The horse's rider is called _____ and _____. We know He is coming to judge sin because of the words in verse 12: His _____ like _____. His right to rule is seen by what is on his Head: many _____.

make YOUR choice

What name of God can I call on when everything seems to be going wrong (v. 16)? "_____ of _____ and _____ of _____"

friday Revelation 19:17-21

take the challenge

What do you think will happen when the beast and the kings of the earth and their armies gather to make war against the rider on the white horse (Jesus Christ)?

CHECK IT OUT

The angel calls the _____ of the air to come and gather for the great supper of God, because there will be more than the vultures can eat! What happens to the beast and the false prophets (v. 20)? _____ and cast/thrown alive into a _____ _____. What was it that killed the armies? The _____ that came out of the mouth of the One riding the white _____

make YOUR choice

Why is it important for me to obey God regardless of what other people do?

_____

_____

_____

saturday Revelation 20:1-6

take the challenge

We will reign with Christ for a millennium. Did you know a millennium is 1000 years?

CHECK IT OUT

Who is the dragon (give three different names for him)?

(1)_____, (2)_____,

(3)_____ What did the angel throw

him into? The _____ _____

Those who have been beheaded for their testimony for Jesus

will be what (v. 6)? P_____ of G_____ and

make YOUR choice

of C_____

What is one of the rewards that I will receive for believing in Jesus?

_____

wyk.

18

Cross out the things you wouldn't want to be caught doing when Jesus comes back again:

witnessing - lying - gossiping

praying - fighting - stealing

worshipping - helping others

complaining

SUNDAY Revelation 20:7-15

take the challenge

What will happen to Satan after his 1,000 years in prison?

CHECK IT OUT

Put the events that took place at the great white throne in order.

____ The sea gave up the dead.

____ Whoever's name was not written in the book was thrown into the Lake of Fire.

____ Each person was judged according to his works.

____ He saw the dead great and small.

____ The dead were judged.

____ Death and Hades were thrown into the Lake of Fire.

____ Another book was opened.

____ Each person was judged according to his works.

make YOUR choice

Can I rejoice because my name is written in the Book of Life? **Yes / No** If not, then the time has come for me to trust Jesus Christ and get out of the world and into the family of God. (Talk to a Christian you know now.)

MONDAY Revelation 21:1-8

take the challenge

Are you ready for a totally new heaven and earth?

CHECK IT OUT

Who does verse 8 say will be in the fiery lake of burning sulfur? _____

_____ _____

_____ _____

_____ _____

This is called "the s_____ d_____".

make YOUR choice

What am I depending on to get me to Heaven? _____

_____ Why not share the Gospel with

someone who's heading for Hell?

TUESDAY Revelation 21:9-16

take the challenge

Who is the bride or wife of the Lamb? You might be surprised.

CHECK IT OUT

Name three really neat things you look forward to seeing in the New Jerusalem, the Holy City of God:

(1)_____

(2)_____

(3)_____

make YOUR choice

Someone I am looking forward to seeing in Heaven is:

_____

85

WEDNESDAY Revelation 21:17-27

take the challenge

What's the most beautiful thing you've ever seen? Just think, Heaven's even more beautiful!

CHECK IT OUT

The foundations of the New Jerusalem are made of precious gems and jewels. List six of them:

1 _____   4 _____

2 _____   5 _____

3 _____   6 _____

make YOUR choice

My name **is / is not** written in the L_____'s

B_____ of L_____(v.27).

thursday Revelation 22:1-7

take the challenge

What do you think the River of the Water of Life is?

CHECK IT OUT

How would you describe the River of Life? Where did it come from and what grew on each side of it? _____

_____

_____

What are some things that will be no more in Heaven?

(1)_____ (v. 3)

(2)_____ (v.5)

make YOUR choice

I will never have to be afraid of the dark in Heaven because _____ will be my _____!

friday — Revelation 22:8-15

take the challenge

What's the first thing you think you'll do when you see Jesus in Heaven?

CHECK IT OUT

What did John do when he had heard and seen these things? _____

What did Jesus ("the Angel") actually call Himself in verse 13? _____ and _____,

the _____ and the _____,

the _____ and the _____.

make YOUR choice

Why is it important for me to learn God's Word?

_____

_____

saturday — Revelation 22:16-21

take the challenge

Just think, someday you'll actually be in Heaven! WOW!

CHECK IT OUT

How did Jesus describe Himself in verse 16? The _____ and _____ of David and the Bright _____ _____ _____ What three people were invited to "Come!" by God's Spirit (v. 17)?

(1)_____ (2) _____

(3) _____

make YOUR choice

Why should I be ready and anxious for the Lord Jesus to come back?

_____

87

wk. 19

Chart Your Course

Solomon – the man who had it all! He was one of the wealthiest kings who ever lived, but there was an amazing secret to his wealth. See if you can find it around the treasure box below.

W S O d m i

SUNDAY 1 Kings 1:15-18, 29-37

take the challenge

Have you ever made a promise to someone?

CHECK IT OUT

Fill in the blanks to find out what happened in today's passage. King D _ _ _ _ promised his wife B _ _ _ _ _ _ _ _, that their son S _ _ _ _ _ _ _ would be the next king after he died. What did Zadok the priest and Nathan the prophet have to do to show the people that Solomon was to be the next king (v. 34)? _____
_____

King David kept his promise even though someone else was trying to become king.

make YOUR choice

How am I at keeping my promises? _____ Do I make silly promises that I cannot possibly keep? _____
Does this honor God?_____How can I honor God with promises I make?_____

MONDAY 1 Kings 2:1-12

take the challenge
Do your parents ever give you advice or instruction about something important?

CHECK IT OUT
What do you do when your parents give you advice? (Circle one.)
listen - think about something else - pretend to listen - ignore them
What good advice did David give his son Solomon in verse 3?

"_____

_____

_____ "

make YOUR choice
Whom should I go to first when I have a problem? _____
God has given me the parents that he wants me to have. I need to take time now to thank God for them!

TUESDAY 1 Kings 3:1-15

take the challenge
If you could have anything in the world, what would you ask for?

CHECK IT OUT
God told Solomon to ask for WHATEVER HE WANTED and God would give it to him! What did King Solomon ask for in verse 9?_____

Was God pleased by his request? **Y / N** What other things did God promise to give to Solomon even though he didn't ask for them? _____

_____

_____

make YOUR choice
What would I like God to give me most of all? _____

_____

Would God be pleased with this request?_____

WEDNESDAY 1 Kings 3:16-28

Cut the baby in half!

Wow! Would you have liked to have been in King Solomon's court the day these two ladies came to visit? How did King Solomon figure out who the living baby belonged to? _____
_____
_____

How did he know who the real mother was?_____
_____

make YOUR choice

Have I told my mom lately that I love her? **Y / N** I will write her a note and tell her these three things I especially appreciate about her: _____ _____ _____

Now I will put it on her pillow so she finds it.

thursday 1 Kings 4:20-34

take the challenge

What would you need in order to rule a kingdom?

CHECK IT OUT

King Solomon needed a lot of things to rule his kingdom and keep all the people happy. Find out some of the things that the king had in this word search! Find these words in the puzzle: **people, horses, straw, flour, barley, cattle, wisdom, sheep, land**

```
P S O F S E S R O H
E W H O M E H W B A
O N I O D O E A A P
P E O S D L E R R P
L R O S D P P T L Y
E X I Q R O E S E N
E L T T A C M R Y B
T L A N D R U O L F
```

I can be a leader and help others if I am willing to seek God for His

_____, _____ and_____.

Who in my life looks up to me to lead the way? _____

friday 1 Kings 6:1-14, 38

ON AIR

take the challenge

News Flash!
Temple Completed!

CHECK IT OUT

Pretend you are a news reporter doing a news report on King Solomon finishing the temple. Fill in the following facts: What material did they use to make the temple roof? _____ Were any tools used in its building? (Read carefully!) _____ What year and month was the temple completed? _____ How many years did it take King Solomon to build the temple?_____

make YOUR choice

Have I ever finished a project that I worked really hard on? _____
How did I feel?_____ How did King Solomon probably feel after finishing God's House?_____

saturday 1 Kings 11:1-13

take the challenge

When you are making an important decision, do you consider all the consequences?

CHECK IT OUT

What happens if you don't obey God and His Word?

_____

There are consequences for our sin. What did King Solomon do that made God very sad? (vv. 9-10)

_____

_____

What was the punishment for Solomon's sin (vv.11-13)?

_____

make YOUR choice

God wants me to follow Him with my whole heart! Circle some things that God wants me to do: confess my sin - be truthful - read His Word - memorize His Word - sing praises to Him. How many did you circle?_____ All these things are ways that I can obey God!

91

20

There are lots of OPPOSITES in our chapters this week! Opposites are things that are different from each other – things that are against each other. Can you draw lines between the opposites of each other below?

Good

judgement

wise

foolish

blessing

destroy

evil

build

bad advice

SUNDAY 1 Kings 11:41-12:15

take the challenge

CHECK IT OUT

Good Advice... Bad Advice...

Solomon died, and his son, Rehoboam, succeeded him as king. The people wanted their workload lightened by the new king. He got advice from two places: his Dad's mature advisors and his own young friends. What was the advice from the older men (v. 7)? _____ _____ What was the advice from the younger men (v.11)? _____ Whose advice did he take?_____ Did the people like this?_____

make your choice

From whom do I listen to and get advice ?_____ _____ Do I REALLY LISTEN when older people who care about me give me advice?_____ Write here the names of two adults I can go to for wise counsel or advice? _____ and _____

MONDAY 1 Kings 12:16-30

take the challenge

Would you worship a cow?

CHECK IT OUT

The people didn't like _____, so they made his brother, _____, king instead. Jeroboam was afraid the people would not stay loyal to him, so he set up his own places of worship. What did the idols look like that he set up?_____ In what two cities did he set them up?_____ and _____
Why did he say the people should worship his idols (v.28)?

_____

_____

make YOUR choice

An idol is anything that one puts before God in his life. Do I have idols in my life?
Yes/No What in my life might I be making MORE IMPORTANT than my relationship with Jesus? (Be honest!)_____
Ask God right now to help you keep Him first in your life.

TUESDAY 1 Kings 13:1-10

take the challenge

A strange message for the king!

CHECK IT OUT

A man of God was sent to give the king a message. Use the code to decipher the message:

A	B	D	E	H	I	J	L	M	N	O	R	S	W
1	2	3	4	5	6	7	8	9	10	11	12	13	14

__ __ __ __ __ __ __ __ __ __ __ __ __ __
1   13 11 10   10 1 9 4 3   7 11 13 6 1 5

__ __ __ __ __ __ __ __ __ __ __ .
14 6 8 8   2 4   2 11 12 10

make YOUR choice

How do I react when I receive news that something will be different than I imagined or wanted? _____
I need to make sure I listen to those who love me when they say no to me...It is usually for my own good or protection!

WEDNESDAY 1 Kings 13:11-25

take the challenge

Obey your orders!

CHECK IT OUT

The man of God was told by God not to e _ _ or d _ _ _ _ until he returned home. Why did he go with the other man if he was told not to eat or drink? _____

What happened to the man of God because he disobeyed God? _____

make YOUR choice

Do you think the prophet who lied to the man of God knew what would happen to him? _____ Do I tell "little white lies" sometimes? _____ Can I get others into trouble with my lies?_____ (Ask God to help you to be truthful in all things.)

thursday 1 Kings 16:29-17:7

take the challenge

Good versus Evil

CHECK IT OUT

This is a classic battle of good versus evil. Fill in the blanks from today's passage.

GOOD	EVIL
God's Man: E _ _ _ _ _ _	Evil king: A _ _ _
His message: There will be no r _ _ _.	Evil wife: J _ _ _ _ _ _ _
False god: B _ _ _	Lived by a b _ _ _ _.
Fed by r _ _ _ _ _.	

make YOUR choice

Am I on the "good" side (God's side) like Elijah? **Yes / No** Have I asked Jesus to be my Savior from sin? Yes/No If no, why not ask your parents or leaders what it means to be God's child today?

friday 1 Kings 17:8-24

take the challenge

Why do bad things happen to "good" people?

CHECK IT OUT

Circle the right answers: The widow in our reading today was doing a (**good / bad**) thing. She was making (**pots / bread**) for Elijah each day. Her supply of oil and flour (**ran out / stayed the same**) as she served the man of God. Her _____ got sick and stopped breathing. Elijah _____ for her son and he (**lived / died**). Bad things sometimes happen to God's people to increase their (**money / faith**) in Him.

make YOUR choice

Have I had something hard happen to me recently? Write it here:

_____

What did God teach me about Himself because of this? _____

_____

saturday 1 Kings 18:1-16

take the challenge

Have you ever been in trouble and said "My mom's going to kill me!"?

CHECK IT OUT

As for the above question, even though you may have been punished, you knew your life was safe. Obadiah had gone against the evil King Ahab, and had hidden _ _ _ prophets of God in caves. He also brought them f _ _ _ and w _ _ _ _. Elijah asked him to tell _____ that he was here to meet him. _____ feared the King would kill him...but Elijah assured him he would be safe.

make YOUR choice

Am I afraid when I think God might want me to do something hard for Him? What hard thing is God asking me to do this week?

_____

_____

Chart Your Course

This week's scripture passages read like an exciting action movie! Who are the characters? What will happen next? Who lives and who dies? Read on and find out from God's exciting Word!

SUNDAY 1 Kings 18:17-29

take the challenge

I challenge you to a bake off...with no fire!

CHECK IT OUT

Elijah is out to prove that God is the ONLY, ONE TRUE _____! He challenges the _____ of _____ to see if their god can start a _____ on the wood and sticks they have set up on the _____. In the space below fill in some of the things Elijah said to the prophets of Baal as they were calling to him: _____

_____

make YOUR choice

How do I know that my God is the one, true God? _____

_____

Take time right now to praise God for allowing you to know HIM, the only ONE TRUE GOD!

MONDAY 1 Kings 18:30-40

take the challenge

CHECK IT OUT

Elijah's turn!

Today is math day! Add up how many jars of water were poured on the Lord's altar:

4 ![jar] + 4 ![jar] + 4 ![jar] =

_____ ![jar] **poured on the altar.**

make YOUR choice

What happened when Elijah prayed (v.38)?

_____

My God is powerful! What do I need my powerful God to help me with this week?_____

TUESDAY 1 Kings 18:41-19:7

take the challenge

The best take-out food ever!

CHECK IT OUT

Elijah was exhausted from his journey and his battle with the prophets of Baal. What neat things did God do for him?

How did he get to Jezreel? _____

What did he eat?_____

Who made it?_____

make YOUR choice

Do I ever get overwhelmed by life?_____ What is stressing me out lately? _____

God gave Elijah the best "rest formula" ever: Get a good night's sleep, eat well, and talk to God! He will help me when I am feeling overwhelmed!

WEDNESDAY 1 Kings 19:8-21

What is God like?

Elijah was going to actually get to speak to the Holy God! Several things happened before Elijah got to talk to God. Maybe Elijah thought that God would be like these other forces of nature. Unscramble the letters to find the things that appeared to Elijah: **DNWI** _____ **QEKRHTAUEA** _____ **REIF** _____

How did God speak to Elijah? He spoke to him in a _____.

Just as Elijah met with God and talked to Him, I can do this, too! Today I want to talk to God about _____ _____. Take time to do it right now!

thursday 1 Kings 21:1-16

Have you ever seen someone pout or whine about something they didn't get?

King _____ is acting like a spoiled, little child! Even though he is king, and can have practically anything he wants, he sulks and is sad that a man won't give him his _____! His wife, J __ __ __ __ __ __ , plots an evil plan to get N __ __ __ __ __ , the man who owns the vineyard, killed.

How do I react when I don't get my way or something that I want? _____ _____ Do I throw a temper tantrum or sulk and give my parents the silent treatment? Does this please God? **Yes/No** Take time to pray this prayer from your heart to God: *God, please help me to react in the right way when I don't get my way this week. Amen*

 **friday** 1 Kings 21:17-29

Dogs will lick your blood!

CHECK IT OUT

The Lord is displeased by Ahab and Jezebel's terrible act. Elijah is sent to give them a scary message in verses 21-23. Summarize it here: _____
_____

How does Ahab react to Elijah's message from God in verse 27? _____ Because of this, what did God decide to do in verse 29? _____
_____

make YOUR choice

Even the most evil person can receive God's mercy if they truly humble themselves before God and repent of their sin. A sinful person that I would like to see come to Christ for salvation is: _____
Pray for them now!

saturday 1 Kings 22:29-40

take the challenge

God means what He says!

 CHECK IT OUT

What did God tell Elijah would happen to Ahab - that comes true in this passage (v. 38)?

_____ How did King Ahab

try to avoid being killed?_____

Did it work? _____

make YOUR choice

God has numbered the days we are to live on this earth. None of us knows how many days we have! That's why it is so important to be sure we know Jesus as our Savior! Do I know Jesus? If yes, write when I accepted Jesus here: _____
_____

If I'm not sure, why not ask my parents or a leader about it today?

wk. 22

WEEKLY PASSAGES COVERED
2 Kings 1:1-5:16

During the time of 2 Kings, the nation of Israel had been divided like this:

NORTHERN KINGDOM
Israel
Capital City: Samaria
19 Bad Kings
Conquered by Assyria

SOUTHERN KINGDOM
Judah
Capital City: Jerusalem
12 Bad Kings
& 8 Good Kings
Conquered by Babylon

God allowed BOTH kingdoms to be conquered because of their sin!

SUNDAY 2 Kings 1:1-18

take the challenge

Where do you go for advice and wisdom?

CHECK IT OUT

Ahaziah the king was injured. Who did he consult about his injury? _____, the _____ of Ekron. God showed how He felt about being ignored by what He did to the king's soldiers in verses 10 and 12. What happened to the soldiers? _____ What happened to Ahaziah (vv. 16b-17)?_____

make YOUR choice

I will get my advice from: ____ **TV shows** ____ **Athletes** ____ **Magazines** ____ **Friends** ____ **Teachers who don't know the Lord** ____ **God's Holy Word** ____ **Godly grown-ups**

Chart Your Course

100

MONDAY 2 Kings 2:1-11

take the challenge

How do you feel when a teacher or someone you look up to moves away?

CHECK IT OUT

To what three places did Elisha follow Elijah?

_____, _____, _____

Did Elisha know that Elijah was going away? _____

What did he ask Elijah for before he left?

_____

make YOUR choice

When someone I love goes away, I will try to _____

_____ all I have learned from them.

TUESDAY 2 Kings 2:12-22

take the challenge

Do you put your trust in people or in God?

CHECK IT OUT

God used Elisha to do two miracles in this chapter, after his master had gone. In verse 14, what did God do to the Jordan River? _____

In verse 21, what did God do to the spring at Jericho?

_____

make YOUR choice

Think of a pastor or teacher you admire, and fill in his name in this sentence: Just like God uses _____,
I can trust Him to give me strength and use me.

WEDNESDAY 2 Kings 4:1-17

take the challenge

Are you ever afraid that you won't have something you need?

CHECK IT OUT

God took care of the prophet's widow by supplying her

with lots of _____ to sell. God took care of Elisha by

giving him a place to _____ in Shunem.

make YOUR choice

One thing that I need right now is _____.

I will pray and trust God to provide it at the right time.

thursday 2 Kings 4:18-37

take the challenge

Can you say "It's okay" even when bad things happen?

CHECK IT OUT

What happened to the son in this passage?_____

_____ His mother answered two different people,

"It will be okay." (**It's all right /It will be well/It shall be

well.**) Can you find the two verses where she said this?

_____ and _____ What did the boy do before he

opened his eyes?_____

make YOUR choice

These verses show me that I can _____

God even when bad things happen.

 **friday** 2 Kings 4:38-44

 take the challenge

What's for dinner?

CHECK IT OUT

When Elisha returned to Gilgal, what bad thing was in

the land or region? _____

What two types of food does God provide in this

passage? _____ and _____

make YOUR choice

When I eat, I will remember who provides my food and

_____ _____ God for it!

saturday 2 Kings 5:1-16

take the challenge

Do you know where to send someone for help?

CHECK IT OUT

Complete the crossword puzzle using these clues!

1. The name of the commander of the army of Syria (or Aram).
2. The disease that the commander had
3. The servant girl was from what country?
4. Who was called the "man of God"?
5. The muddy river Naaman was told to wash in
6. The number of times Naaman was told to wash in the river

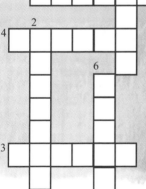

make YOUR choice

Like the servant girl, I want to be able to help people, by sending

them to _____, the only One who can cure the

disease of sin.

23

"UNCLEAN! UNCLEAN!"

In Israel, people who had the terrible disease of leprosy had to call out these words whenever someone came too close to them, in order to keep the disease from spreading to others. Leprosy caused terrible sores on the skin, and fingers and toes would literally fall off. And there was no cure for it. (Did you know that there are still people in third world countries today who have this awful disease?)

SUNDAY 2 Kings 5:17-27

take the challenge

The best seat...The biggest piece of pizza....that sounds greedy! Read about Greedy Gehazi!

CHECK IT OUT

Elisha had refused any reward for his part in Naaman's healing, but his servant, Gehazi, chased after Naaman and asked for what (vv. 21-23)? _____ and _____ Read verse 25. Did he tell Elisha the truth?_____ What was his punishment for greed and lying?_____

_____

make YOUR choice

What have I not been content with, but wishing that I had more of? Lord, help me not to be g_____, but instead to be content with what You provide for me. And help me always to tell the t_____ .

MONDAY 2 Kings 6:1-7

take the challenge

Can metal float? (Put a quarter into a sink of water and find out!)

CHECK IT OUT

What were the prophets doing?_____ _____ Who went with them?_____ _____ What did they lose in the water?_____ What did the man of God do to help them find it? _____

make YOUR choice

Is God interested in the ordinary problems of my ordinary life? _____ He has the power to help me when things go wrong? _____

TUESDAY 2 Kings 6:8-23

take the challenge

Have you ever felt like you were outnumbered and overpowered?

CHECK IT OUT

Verse 15 - What was the servant afraid of? _____

Verse 17 - What did he see when the Lord opened his eyes? _____ _____

make YOUR choice

I will write down and try to memorize what Elisha said in verse 16 to encourage me when I feel afraid: "_____ _____ _____ " 105

WEDNESDAY 2 Kings 6:24-33

The word "famine" means "a great shortage of food."

Verse 25 says that food was very:
expensive / cheap (circle one)

Verse 29 says that people were so hungry they were eating: **trash / other people** (circle one)

Thinking about how hungry those people were should make me very _____ for what I have to eat.
Pray today for children all over the world who have nothing to eat.
Pray for the missionaries who are trying to help them.

thursday 2 Kings 7:1-11

When you receive a great blessing, do you keep it to yourself?

Match the event with the verse where you find it recorded by drawing lines between them.

- Elisha predicts an abundant supply of inexpensive food.

Verse 6

- Syrians (Arameans) flee from their camp because of a vision from the Lord.

Verse 8

- Lepers find plenty to eat in the Syrian camp.

Verses 1 & 2

Verse 19

- Lepers share their good news with the gatekeepers.

A blessing I want to share with my friends is_____

_____.

friday 2 Kings 7:12-20

take the challenge

What must you have to experience God's fullest blessing?

CHECK IT OUT

Number the following events in today's passage in the correct order:

_____ Two chariots with horses are sent to chase after the Syrian (Aramean) army.

_____ The gatekeeper didn't believe Elisha's prediction about God providing plenty of food for all.

_____ The Syrians (Arameans) left to hide in the fields and countryside.

_____ The ones sent find an abundance of clothing, equipment and food items left all over by the enemy when they had run away (fled).

_____ The gatekeeper is trampled in the gate and dies.

make YOUR choice

Is there a promise in God's Word that I have doubted or not really wanted to believe? *Lord, help my faith grow as I learn to believe all of your promises, unlike the Samarian gatekeeper.*

saturday 2 Kings 9:1-10

take the challenge

How does God destroy evil in the world?

CHECK IT OUT

Who was anointed to be king? _____

What two evil people was this king to destroy?

A_____ and J_____

Who has been hurt by these people (v. 7)?

_____

make YOUR choice

What evil or bad habit in my life do I need to fight today and get victory over with God's help? _____

Lord, I know You hate evil because of how it hurts Your people. Help me to be strong against evil.

Take a look at some of the consequences of Israel's sin:

Exile (being taken away from home to live in a strange place)

Sickness & death

Fire from heaven

Wars

Famine (a shortage of food)

What consequences of sin can you see in our world today?

SUNDAY 2 Kings 13:14-21

take the challenge

When you are sick, what do you want to do?

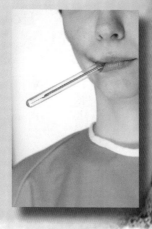

CHECK IT OUT

Circle the things Elisha did while he was sick:

Complained about the food

Cried because his head hurt

Encouraged the king

Gave the king advice

make YOUR choice

The next time I am sick, I will remember Elisha's example and try to

_____

_____ .

MONDAY 2 Kings 17:6-23

When you decide to disobey, do you think about the consequences of your disobedience?

The people of Israel were taken away from their homes to what country?_____ Why did this happen (v. 7)?_____
_____ What were some of the sins Israel committed? - Worshipped_____
- Sold themselves to do_____ - Provoked the Lord to _____ - Like their fathers, did not _____in the Lord their God.

I don't want to make God angry. I will carefully _____ about

what is right and what is wrong before I make choices about what to do.

TUESDAY 2 Kings 17:24-41

Is God pleased when you say that you love Him, but make up your own rules?

True or False

_____ Priests came to teach people how to worship the Lord.

_____ The people started worshipping the Lord.

_____ The people worshipped their own gods in their own way.

_____ God was pleased for them to keep their old religious

customs, as long as they worshipped Him, too.

Do I please God on the ball field and at school as much as I please Him at church? _____ Why or why not? _____
_____

WEDNESDAY 2 Kings 19:5-20

take the challenge

When you hear that bad things are happening, what do you do?

CHECK IT OUT

_____, God's messenger, said "Do not be afraid of what you have heard." _____ _____, an enemy, sent letters saying that Assyria was destroying all the countries. Hezekiah talked to _____ and asked Him to _____ them.

make YOUR choice

When I am afraid and don't know what to do, I will _____ _____ like Hezekiah did.

thursday 2 Kings 19:35-20:11

take the challenge

Every sickness is an opportunity for healing!

CHECK IT OUT

What did Hezekiah do when he was very sick?
1. _____ to the Lord 2. _____ very much (bitterly)

Isaiah brought God's answer: " I have heard your _____ and seen your _____. I will _____ you."

make YOUR choice

What is a prayer of mine that God has answered? _____ What am I especially praying for now? _____ _____

friday 2 Kings 20:12-21

take the challenge Is it always smart to tell everything you know?

CHECK IT OUT Draw lines from each question to the correct answer.

- Where Hezekiah's visitors came from
- What the visitors brought
- What Hezekiah showed to them
- This is what Hezekiah was when he didn't care how his bragging would affect his children

Selfish

All of his riches

Babylon

A get well gift

make YOUR choice I will THINK and PRAY about it before I _____

_____.

saturday 2 Kings 22:3-10 and 23:1-3

take the challenge Can you imagine having no Bible for 26 years of your life?

CHECK IT OUT Josiah organized a big project to repair the

_____. What did they find in

the temple? _____

What did the king do with the book? _____

_____

make YOUR choice

I have my own copy of God's Word. **YES / NO**

I greatly value God's Word. **YES / NO**

I read God's Word every day. **YES / NO**

I honor God's Word by obeying what I read there. **YES / NO**

25

Did You Know...

"Omniscient" (om-nish-ent) means "all-knowing?"

The fruit of a fig tree is hidden in the leaves until it is ripe?

"Omnipotent" (om-nip-po-tent) means "all-powerful?"

Nicodemus was a Pharisee?

A Pharisee was a religious leader?

SUNDAY John 1:1-14

take the challenge

Have you ever had an important job to do? What was it?

CHECK IT OUT

What was John's important job (v. 7)? _____

_____

Who do you believe "the light" is in verse 7? _____

_____

make YOUR choice

If I have accepted "the True Light" (Jesus) as my Savior, I need to tell someone about it today. If I haven't trusted Jesus, why not ask Him to save me from my sins today?

MONDAY John 1:15-28

 Have you ever watched the news on TV? How does a reporter get answers?

How did John answer the question "who are you" (v. 20)?_____ Who did he say he was (v. 23)?_____

_____

make YOUR choice

If someone asked me about Jesus, what would I say? _____

_____

_____

TUESDAY John 1:29-42

take the challenge What are five things you love about your room?

 Why do you think the disciples wanted to know where Jesus was staying (v. 38)?

_____

_____

The disciples were so excited to meet Jesus that they wanted to spend the whole day with Him!

make YOUR choice

I can spend some time with Jesus in my home by doing my Q_____ T_____ each day.

WEDNESDAY John 1:43-51

take the challenge

Do you have a favorite tree in your yard? Circle what you do with your tree. Climb It / Build a tree house in it / Eat its fruit / Relax in its shade

CHECK IT OUT

Did Nathaniel believe in Jesus right away (v. 46)? Jesus told Nathaniel what he was doing before Philip brought him, and he was amazed. Jesus could do this. Remember Jesus is God the Son and He is _____ _____. (Hint: Pick a word from Chart Your Course, which means "all knowing".)

make your choice

If God is omniscient, what can I hide from Him? _____

thursday John 2:1-12

take the challenge

Have you ever been to a wedding? What did you like about it?

CHECK IT OUT

What ran out at this wedding?

_____

Jesus performed His first miracle at this wedding. What was the miracle?

_____

make your choice

This miracle showed that Jesus is _____. (Check out Chart Your Course.) How can I trust His power to help me today? _____

friday John 2:13-25

take the challenge

What do you do when you are mad about something?

CHECK IT OUT

Why was Jesus angry?
Jesus' anger was not sin because He was angry at what the people were doing wrong. When we get angry, we often are mad because someone has done something we didn't like. This is SIN. It is okay to be angry at injustice or sin, but not at little things people do to bother us.

make YOUR choice

Stop and think when you are mad: Am I angry at sin? If the answer is "No", I need to take time to tell God I am sorry

saturday John 3:1-12

take the challenge

When is your physical birthday? What about your spiritual one?

CHECK IT OUT

What did Jesus tell Nicodemus he had to do to get to Heaven (v. 3)?

"You must be _____ _____!"

make YOUR choice

"Born again" means to accept Jesus as your Savior - the only One who can save you from your sin. Write a sentence about when you were "born again". (If you haven't been born again by accepting Jesus, talk to your parents, leader, or Sunday School teacher about it.) _____

_____ 115

Chart Your Course

26

"Humility" means "not thinking too highly of yourself" – "not proud."

The Jews disliked Samaritans so much that they would take a longer route to avoid their country.

A miracle is something only God can do that will bring glory to His name.

SIN - the wrong things we do, say, or think; anything that goes against God's Word.

SUNDAY   John 3:13-24

take the challenge

Have you ever watched a football game on TV? Sometimes people hold up a card with the most famous Bible verse in the world written on it.

CHECK IT OUT

The most familiar verse of all is found in this passage. It is John 3:16. It says that __ __ __ loved the world (us) so much that He gave His only __ __ __ to die for us.

make YOUR choice

Have I made the decision to accept Jesus as my Savior? If I haven't, why not today? If you have accepted Jesus, share your faith with others.

MONDAY John 3:25-36

Can you think of a time when you had a fight with someone about who was better?

John the Baptist's followers were concerned because many people were following Jesus. John shows his humility (see Chart Your Course) by his answer in verse 30. Write it here: _____

_____

make YOUR choice

John the Baptist said his job was to point people to Jesus.
Circle how I can do this in my life.
Whine / Pray / Complain / Read the Bible / Get mad

TUESDAY John 4:1-15

take the challenge

What do you do when you are thirsty? It's easy to get a drink when you want one, isn't it?

Jesus stopped to talk to a woman at a _____.
Every day she would have to come to the _____
two times to get _____. Most Jewish men wouldn't
have talked to her because she was a sinful woman.
Jesus is different; He loves all people, and wants to
forgive their sin. Jesus had _____ water to offer her.

make YOUR choice

Is there someone I don't like or can't get along with? **Yes / No**
I will add their name to my prayer list now and pray for them.

WEDNESDAY John 4:16-30

take the challenge

What part of the church worship service do you like best?

CHECK IT OUT

The woman was asking Jesus about where to worship. Jesus said that He wants us to worship **how** (v. 24)?

In S _ _ _ _ _ _ and

T _ _ _ _ _

make YOUR choice

Jesus told her the most important part of worship was her heart attitude. What does God see in **my** heart when I worship Him? _____

thursday John 4:31-42

take the challenge

Have you ever seen a vegetable garden harvested? The farmer or gardener knows when the vegetables are just right to pick.

CHECK IT OUT

Jesus compared telling others about Him to a harvest field. He said (v. 34), "My _____ is to do the _____ of Him who _____ me." When people share the Gospel, sometimes people will trust Jesus. Sometimes they won't. Our job is to be faithful to tell others about Jesus.

make YOUR choice

I will pray for God to bring someone across my path with whom I can share the Gospel. Remember — John 3:16.

 # John 4:43-54

take the challenge

Can you think of a time when you had a fever or were sick? Were your parents worried? How did you feel?

CHECK IT OUT

The son of a royal official was very sick — even dying. With one spoken phrase, Jesus healed the boy. Write the words He said here: "_____." This was a miracle! (See Chart Your Course.)

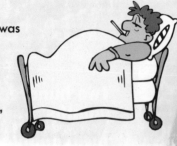

make YOUR choice

We serve a POWERFUL God! He can do all things! Here are three things I can praise Him for: 1)_____,
2)_____, 3)_____

saturday John 5:1-14

take the challenge

Have you seen or do you know someone in a wheelchair? How do you think it would feel if you couldn't walk?

CHECK IT OUT

Another miracle! Jesus made the _____ man _____. He healed him physically. But the man also needed spiritual healing — he needed to have his _____ forgiven (v. 14). (See Chart Your Course.)

make YOUR choice

If I know Jesus as my Savior I need to "tell on myself" to God whenever I sin. I John 1:9 tells me how. I'll write it here, then ask God to forgive me right away when I sin: "_____
_____"

27

Did you know the phrase, "What would Jesus do?" (WWJD) is taken from a book called *In His Steps* by Charles Sheldon.

Two hundred denarii was about eight months' wages.

Jesus fulfilled every Old Testament prophecy about the coming Messiah – yet the Jewish people still would not believe in Him.

SUNDAY John 5:15-27

Do you look like your mom or your dad? Do people tell you that you look like one or the other?

Jesus was calling _____ His _____, making Himself _____ with God (v. 18). Jesus proved that He was God the Son through His sinless life, His miracles, and His death on the cross and resurrection.

make YOUR choice

Because of His oneness with God, Jesus lived as God wanted Him to live. WWJD has become a catch phrase, but is also a phrase that I need to ask myself every day... What Would Jesus Do in this situation? I need to think about these words before I act!

MONDAY John 5:28-38

take the challenge

Can you think of a time when someone thought you weren't being truthful — but then someone else backed up your story?

CHECK IT OUT

Jesus is again telling the Jews that He is equal with God the Father, and this time He tells them that _____ (v. 33) is His witness. He says that this man was like a (circle one): **strong lion/ fisherman/ shining lamp or light.**

make YOUR choice

It's true! Jesus is God's Son! Every week my pastor and Sunday school teacher back up this truth. How can I let them know how much I appreciate them? Could I write one of them a special thank you letter to show my appreciation?

TUESDAY John 5:39-47

take the challenge

Have you ever hoped and wished for something that never happened? Were you disappointed?

CHECK IT OUT

The Jews were hoping and waiting for a Savior, but they would not believe in Jesus. Jesus said that Moses wrote about Him. He did this in Deuteronomy 18:15. Look up this Old Testament verse and write it on the lines provided. "_____

_____

_____"

make YOUR choice

What would I like to have Jesus find me doing if He were to come today?

_____

121

WEDNESDAY John 6:1-14

take the challenge

Can you think of a time when you were really hungry and you had nothing with you to eat?

CHECK IT OUT

Wow! Jesus fed 5,000 people with a boy's lunch! This is another M _ _ _ _ _ _ _. To buy food for that many people would be expensive, but Jesus is all-powerful or _ _ _ _ _ _ _ _ _ _, (see Chart your Course for week 25), and can do anything!

make YOUR choice

I can trust Jesus' power to help me. What do I need help with this week? _____

thursday John 6:15-27

take the challenge

What are you afraid of?

CHECK IT OUT

The disciples were afraid when a storm came up and Jesus was walking on water toward them. But He comforted them with the words in verse 20. Write them below.

" _____

_____

_____

_____ "

make YOUR choice

Whatever I'm afraid of, I need to remember, that if I know Jesus, He is with me always. I can P _ _ _ _ Y to Him when I am afraid. I will pray right now for _____.

friday John 6:28-40

take the challenge

What do you do when you are hungry?

CHECK IT OUT

The people wanted bread so they wouldn't feel hungry. Jesus tells them that He is the "_____ _____ _____" in verse 35. Just like we need to eat food everyday to stay healthy — we also need "spiritual food" everyday to keep our relationship with Jesus strong.

make YOUR choice

Circle what you can do to get "spiritual food" daily.

Pray / Use swear words / Read the Bible Disobey / Confess my sins

saturday John 6:41-58

take the challenge

Have you ever been recognized by another family member like, "That's Joe's son." or "That's Mary's sister." or "She's Sheila's daughter."?

CHECK IT OUT

The Jewish leaders couldn't accept Jesus as God. They kept saying (v. 42) "Isn't this _____ son?" They would not believe that He was Who He said He was. Jesus reminded them in verse 48 (write it out on the slice of bread):

"
_____
_____
_____ "

make YOUR choice

Who is Jesus to **me**? (Write it down - as well as what I believe about Him.) _____
_____

123

wk.

28 Did you know?

The Feast of Tabernacles was a seven-day celebration to help the Israelites remember what God had done for them.

To "stone" someone meant that a person would be killed by rocks that others threw at them.

SUNDAY John 6:59-70

take the challenge

Did you ever know someone who pretended to be your friend, but later they did or said something that hurt you? Were they a true friend?

CHECK IT OUT

All of the 12 disciples believed in Jesus except one.

Jesus knew who was not a true friend or believer in Him.

Who was it? Write his name here: _____

make your choice

My earthly friends will fail me at times, but Jesus is a Friend who will never fail me. Look up Hebrews 13:5. This verse tells me that Jesus will never _____ me or _____me.

MONDAY John 7:1-13

Are you afraid to speak about Jesus to your friends? Is it easy or hard for you to do this?

In these verses everyone is talking about Jesus — but secretly. They wouldn't talk about Him in public. Verse 5 tells us that not even Jesus' own _____ believed in Him. How sad!

How about me? If a friend asked me about my church or youth group, what would I say? Pray this week for someone to witness to. Take the first step.

TUESDAY John 7:14-24

take the challenge

Read the first part of Chart Your Course. This is the feast that is talked about in these verses.

CHECK IT OUT

Jesus began teaching in the temple about halfway through the seven-day feast. What were the Jews so amazed about (v. 15)? _____

_____

_____

_____

make YOUR choice

If I was with my family at this seven-day celebration, what are some things I would remember and thank God for that have happened to me in the past? Write them below and take time to thank God for them.

_____

_____

WEDNESDAY John 7:25-39

take the challenge

Will everyone go to Heaven when they die?

CHECK IT OUT

Many young people think that everyone is a Christian or that everyone will go to Heaven when they die. But in verse 34 Jesus tells unsaved religious people of His day, "Where I am {Heaven} you c_____ c_____."

make YOUR choice

How about me? Have I accepted Jesus as my Savior? If I haven't, why not? What am I waiting for? Don't put this decision off until it is too late!

thursday John 7:40-53

take the challenge

Have you ever been so into what a preacher was talking about that the sermon seemed to "fly by"?

CHECK IT OUT

The temple guards were sent to arrest Jesus, but instead His teaching amazed them. They couldn't find any reason to arrest Him! The people in verses 40 and 41 thought He was either a _____ or "the _____."

make YOUR choice

How do I act when God's Word is being shared? Circle one: **fool around - listen carefully - doodle - write notes to friends - distract others - takes notes on message** Is God pleased? _____

 **friday** John 8:1-11

 take the challenge

Have you ever gotten in trouble at school? Did you feel like everyone else was looking at you?

CHECK IT OUT

The religious leaders brought a sinful woman to Jesus.

They wanted Jesus to "_____" her for her sin.

He turned it around and told them that if any of them

had no _____, he should throw the first _____.

Not surprisingly, they all did what? _____

make YOUR choice

This passage reminds me that (circle one):

All have sinned. / Some have sinned. / Only bad people sin.

---

saturday John 8:12-24

take the challenge

Do you have a flashlight? What do you use it for?

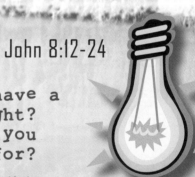

CHECK IT OUT

Jesus called Himself the

L_____ of the W_____ (v. 12)

When we accept Jesus as Savior, He promises to be with us, protect us, and guide us. The bright candles in the temple where Jesus was speaking reminded the people of God's presence, protection, and guidance.

make YOUR choice

What does it mean to follow Jesus and how am I doing? _____

_____

_____ 127

wk.

29

Did You Know...

that "eternal" means "having no ending and no beginning"?

.... that God is eternal – He always was and always will be?

.... that "Siloam" means "sent"?

.... that "attribute" means "trait or characteristic"?

SUNDAY John 8:25-36

take the challenge

How can you show your parents that you love them?

CHECK IT OUT

Jesus says in verse 29, that He _____ did

what _____ His Father, God. When I

obey and please my parents, I also please _____,

my heavenly _____.

make YOUR choice

What are some things I could STOP doing that would please my parents? _____

_____

MONDAY John 8:37-47

Do you love God? How do you show it?

Jesus says that if you belong to God you will listen to and hear what He says.

Do the crossword that shows some ways I can show my love for God.

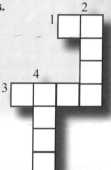

ACROSS

1. _____ to church
3. Talking to God: _____

DOWN

2. To do what you should: _____
4. _____ God's Word

TUESDAY John 8:48-59

Have you ever felt frustrated when you are trying to explain something and no one understands what you are saying?

Jesus was trying to explain who He was to the Jews, but they wouldn't listen. They did not believe that Jesus was the Messiah, and therefore couldn't comprehend what He was saying. In verse 58, He claimed to be the eternal God when He said, "Before _____ was (born), _____ _____." (See Chart Your Course.) Jesus was claiming to be eternal here — the Eternal God — always in existence.

What does it mean to me that Jesus is eternal (see Chart Your Course)? _____

_____ 129

WEDNESDAY John 9:1-12

take the challenge

Have you ever been in a place that was so dark you couldn't see your hand in front of your face?

CHECK IT OUT

Imagine being born blind! The man in this passage was _____ when he _____ Jesus. He went to wash in the pool of _____ (see Chart Your Course) — and he could see! Another miracle!

make YOUR choice

Jesus said that this man was born blind so that the work of God could be displayed in his life (v 3). When I obey God He can work through me — and be glorified in my life.

thursday John 9:13-25

take the challenge

Do you like detective stories with mysteries to solve?

CHECK IT OUT

Pretend you are a reporter. Write five facts from the story in these verses. (1)_____,

(2) _____,

(3) _____,

(4) _____,

(5) _____

make YOUR choice

Share your testimony (how you became a Christian) with your parents or club leader.

 **friday** John 9:26-41

take the challenge

Have you ever told a true story – but no one believed that it was really true?

 CHECK IT OUT

Some _____ would not believe the man's story – that he was _____ and Jesus had _____ him. He was finally _____ out of the synagogue because of his belief in Jesus.

make YOUR choice

When have I ever been made fun of or been made to feel left out because of my belief in Jesus? _____

_____

saturday John 10:1-13

take the challenge

Have you ever touched a sheep? What did it feel like?

 **CHECK IT OUT**

In this passage, Jesus claims to be the _____ _____. Who are the sheep? _____ Look up Psalm 23 to see what the Good Shepherd does. Write down three things He does for me here:

(1) _____

(2) _____

(3) _____

 make YOUR choice

Jesus is the Shepherd who protects, loves and cares for me, His special sheep. How does He show His love for me? _____

_____

wk.

30

Chart Your Course

The shortest verse in the Bible is John 11:35.

It says "Jesus wept." To "weep" means "to cry or sob".

"Omnipotent" means "all-powerful"

Three hundred pence or denarii was about a year's wages.

SUNDAY   John 10:14-30

take the challenge

Do you have a pet? Does it come when you call its name?

CHECK IT OUT

Here, Jesus again calls Himself the Good Shepherd and those who know Him as Savior He calls His _____. In verse 27, Jesus says His "sheep" hear and listen to his V __ __ __ __. We hear Jesus speak to us through his _____.

make your choice

How can I listen to God's voice this week? _____

_____

What is God speaking to me about today? _____

_____

MONDAY John 10:31-42

take the challenge
Sometimes we won't believe something until we see it with our own eyes. Did this ever happen to you?

CHECK IT OUT
The Jews were still trying to make Jesus slip up with His words. They would not believe that He was God's Son. Jesus said that even if they wouldn't believe His _____, they should believe because of His _____.

make YOUR choice
Even though the Jews had seen Jesus' miracles, they still would not believe in Him. What do I believe about Jesus? (Circle below)

He never sinned. / He is God's Son. / He died for me. / He rose from the dead.

TUESDAY John 11:1-15

take the challenge
Have you ever been sick? Was your family worried about you?

CHECK IT OUT
Jesus loved Mary, Martha, and Lazarus very much, so why didn't He come right away when He found out about Lazarus' sickness (v. 4)?

_____

_____

make YOUR choice
Why doesn't God always answer my requests right away?

_____

133

WEDNESDAY John 11:16-29

take the challenge

How can you live forever?

CHECK IT OUT

Jesus tells Martha "I AM THE _____ AND THE _____" (v. 25). He also said that whoever believes in _____ will never _____ (v. 26). This means that we will never be separated from God. When our life on this earth is over, we will live _____ in Heaven with God.

make YOUR choice

How do I know that I will live forever? _____
_____

thursday John 11:30-44

take the challenge

Has someone you loved died? How did you feel?

CHECK IT OUT

Jesus really loved Lazarus and his sisters. When He came to the tomb, He _____. (See Chart Your Course.) At first, everyone was _____ about Lazarus' death, and then they were _____ because Jesus brought him back to life.

make YOUR choice

How can I can be happy in the midst of my sadness? _____
_____
_____

friday John 11:45-57

take the challenge

Have you ever read a book about someone in danger?

CHECK IT OUT

Jesus was in danger. What were the chief priests and Pharisees plotting to do to Jesus (v. 53)? _____

_____

But, remember, Jesus is God the Son! These men could do nothing unless God let them.

make YOUR choice

Jesus is omnipotent. (See Chart Your Course.) All power belongs to Him. If I know Jesus I have His _____ on my side.

saturday John 12:1-12

take the challenge

Think of something that is very expensive. Pretend that it belongs to you.

CHECK IT OUT

Mary worshipped Jesus by giving Him something that was very precious and special to her, and very expensive. (See Chart Your Course.) What was it? _____

make YOUR choice

How can I worship Jesus? (Circle the ways) **Obey Him / Give my life to Him / Serve Him / Tell others about Him / Sing a song of worship to Him**

135

31 Hosanna means Save!

A prophecy is a prediction of something to come.

To predict something means to declare in advance that something will happen.

Washing someone's feet was a job that a household servant would do for guests.

SUNDAY John 12:12-22

take the challenge

CHECK IT OUT

Have you ever ridden on a horse or a donkey?

Jesus fulfilled a prophecy when He rode into Jerusalem on a _____. (See Chart Your Course) Look up and read this prophecy that is found in Zechariah 9:9.

make YOUR choice

The people praised Jesus as He rode into the city. What are some things I can praise Him for today? _____

_____

MONDAY John 12:23-36

Have you ever planted a seed? How did you do it?

Jesus is predicting His death on the cross in verses 23-38. (See Chart Your Course.) He uses the illustration of a kernel or grain of __ __ __ __ __ (v. 24). A seed must _____ and then be buried in the _____ for a plant to grow up and produce more seeds.

Jesus had to die to pay for our sin, but also to show His power over death. He proved He is God by coming back to life. Because He is God, He can give eternal life to all who accept Him as Savior. Have I done this? **Yes/ No**

TUESDAY John 12:37-50

Do you believe in Jesus? Do others know this about you?

There were some leaders in the synagogue who believed in Jesus, but were afraid to tell others. Who were they afraid of (v. 42)? P __ __ __ __ __ __ __ __ __ __ Verse 43 tells us that they loved _____ more than the

_____ .

I should serve God and help others so _____ will get the glory, not so _____ will praise me.

137

WEDNESDAY John 13:1-11

take the challenge

Guess how much Jesus loves you? Is there a limit to His love?

CHECK IT OUT

Verse one tells us that Jesus showed His disciples the full extent of His

_____ by serving them and

ultimately dying on the cross for them and us. What

amazing love! How special you are!

make YOUR choice

Write your name in the blanks.
Jesus loves _____!
_____ is special to God!

thursday John 13:12-20

take the challenge

Do you wear sandals in the summer? Do your feet get dirty?

CHECK IT OUT

In Jesus' day, the people wore sandals and their feet would get dirty on the dusty roads. Jesus showed the disciples that they were to be servants to others by His example of _____ their dirty _____. (See Chart Your Course.) Serving others means putting the interests of others ahead of my own interests.

make YOUR choice

Sometimes I have to do things that are hard and I don't like serving others.
Circle how I can be a servant this week: **Take out the trash / Pick up my brother's dirty clothes / Say, "I'm sorry" first / Dust the furniture**

friday John 13:21-38

Have you ever felt betrayed by one of your friends?

In this passage Jesus tells us who would betray Him.

Who was it (v. 26)? _____ How would he betray

Jesus? _____

_____

make YOUR choice

I can be a loyal friend by _____

_____ .

saturday John 14:1-14

What would it be like to live in a mansion?

Jesus tells us here that in His _____'s

_____ are many _____ .

In Heaven, Jesus is preparing a special place

for all who know Him as Savior.

Sometimes it's scary to think about eternity - but Jesus knows

and loves us best. That's why He tells us not to let our hearts be

t _ _ _ _ _ _ _ _ _ or anxious (v. 1).

w.k.

32

Did You Know...

Chart Your Course

That a grapevine is a fruitful plant?. . .

A single vine produces many grapes?. . .

That in the Passover meal, the fruit of the vine symbolized God's goodness to His people?

SUNDAY John 14:15-24

take the challenge

How do we show God that we love Him?

CHECK IT OUT

Jesus explains how we can show Him that we love Him (v. 15). "If you love me, _____ _____." In verse 21, Jesus tells us that the person who has His _____ and _____ them, is the one who really _____ Him. He then promises that whoever _____ Him will be loved by His _____ and Him.

make YOUR choice

What are some ways I can prove my love for God? _____ _____

MONDAY John 14:25-31

take the challenge

Do you need help with your homework sometimes? Who helps you?

CHECK IT OUT

If we know Jesus as Savior then we have someone to help us understand God's will and God's Word. Who is this Helper (or Comforter) (v. 26)? _____ _____ What are two ways this wonderful Helper will help you?

(1) _____

(2) _____

make YOUR choice

When I am having a hard time understanding what God wants me to do or say — I can pray! Right now I will kneel and ask God the Holy Spirit to be my Helper.

TUESDAY John 15:1-11

take the challenge

Do you like grapes?

CHECK IT OUT

Jesus calls Himself the T __ __ __ V __ __ __ in verse 1.

He wants us to obey Him and put our full faith and trust in Him, so that we can do and have what?

(See verses 5, 7, 8, 10, and 11.) _____

_____

_____

make YOUR choice

How can I be a fruit-bearer for Jesus this week? _____

_____

_____

WEDNESDAY John 15:12-27

take the challenge

How can we be God's friends?

CHECK IT OUT

If we know Jesus as Savior, then He calls us His

_____ (v. 14). Two times (vv. 12, 17), He tells

us His command is for us to _____ each other.

make YOUR choice

What are ways I can get to know my friend, Jesus, better? (Circle below)
Complain - Pray - Read the Bible - "Talk back" to my parents - Memorize verses

thursday John 16:1-11

take the challenge

How do you feel inside when you sin?

CHECK IT OUT

We usually know when we have done something or said something wrong. If we know Jesus as Savior, we have the Holy Spirit living in us to convict us of sin when we do wrong. What are three things Jesus says the Holy Spirit will convict us of (v. 8)? (1) _____,
(2) _____, (3) _____

make YOUR choice

What should I do when I sin? Read 1John 1:9 and write it here.

_____

_____

friday John 16:12-22

Have you ever felt sad? When?

Jesus told the disciples that they would be (circle one)

[mad/ afraid/ sad] when He left earth, but that their

grief or sorrow would be turned to _____ because

they would _____ Him again.

If I know Jesus then I can never be totally sad, because I have joy in my heart that only He can give. How can I share that joy with others? _____

saturday John 16:23-33

Are you ever frightened by world events on the news?

In verse 33, Jesus said that we could have

PEACE in Him.

(Color in with a marker)

If we know Jesus, we don't need to be afraid of what happens or will happen in the world. We need to trust Jesus, and remember what He said in the last five words of verse 33:

"_____ _____ _____ _____ _____."

143

"Unity" means
"oneness or harmony."

Malchus was the name of the servant whose ear Peter cut off.

Luke 22:51 tells us that Jesus healed Malchus' ear.

Jesus was crucified at a place called "Golgotha" which means "the place of the skull."

SUNDAY John 17:1-13

take the challenge

How do we know what is true?

CHECK IT OUT

Jesus is praying in these verses. He is praying for you, if you know Him as your Savior. How do we know that God is true? His Word tells us in verse 3 that God is the O_____ T_____ G_____. He says that to know Him is _____ _____.

make YOUR choice

How can I know what is true and right? _____

_____

MONDAY John 17:14-26

take the challenge

How will the world know we are Christians?

CHECK IT OUT

If we want to show Jesus' love to others, we must first show love to our fellow _____. Jesus calls this Unity. (See Chart Your Course) If we are always arguing, fighting and complaining amongst ourselves — we won't be showing Jesus' _____.

make YOUR choice

How will I show love in action to my fellow Christians (and non-Christians) today? _____
_____

TUESDAY John 18:1-14

take the challenge

How would you feel if your friend was in trouble?

CHECK IT OUT

Peter drew his sword and cut off a servant's

__ __ __. Jesus told him to put his _____

away. (See Chart Your Course.)

make YOUR choice

Jesus knew He had to die to save us. He called doing God's will "to drink the __ __ __ God gave Him.". How can I know God's will for me? _____

WEDNESDAY John 18:15-27

Are you ever afraid to be known as a Christian?

Peter is asked if he is one of Jesus' _____.

How does he answer (v. 17)? _____

_____

Why is it so hard sometimes for me to tell people about Jesus?

_____

_____

thursday John 18:28-40

Have you ever been blamed for something you didn't do?

Jesus is taken to _____, who finds no reason

to arrest Jesus or sentence Him to _____. But the

Jews want Him to die so badly that a criminal, named

_____, is set free instead of Jesus.

Just like He did for Barabbas, Jesus took my punishment for sin so
I can go to Heaven someday. Because of what my Savior did, I am

_____!

friday John 19:1-11

take the challenge

Who is the most powerful of all?

CHECK IT OUT

_____ thought he held the

power to crucify Jesus or set Him

free. Jesus told him that his power

was given to him by ___ ___ ___.

make YOUR choice

Only God has the power to give or take life. Just like God had a plan for Jesus' life — He has a plan for my life, too! Praise Jesus for the plan He already has for my life!

saturday John 19:12-22

take the challenge

How do you feel when you read the crucifixion story?

CHECK IT OUT

Our love for Jesus should grow when we realize

what He did for us. Write down three things Jesus

did for us when He went to Calvary: (1) _____,

(2) _____, (3) _____

make YOUR choice

I am special! The Bible tells me that God knew me before I was even born. Wow! God must have really loved me if He sent His only Son to die for me. Write how you feel about God's love. _____

_____

147

34

The word "finished" in John 19:30 is the same as "paid in full."

Jesus' tomb was probably a cave carved out of the stone hillside. It was large enough to walk into, and a large stone was rolled in front of the entrance.

The Sabbath day began Friday evening at sundown.

SUNDAY John 19:23-30

take the challenge

Have you ever felt sad?

CHECK IT OUT

Jesus' mother and disciples were very sad when He died. Jesus didn't deserve to die, but He chose to die so that we would have eternal life. Right before He died He said these three words (v. 30), "_____ _____ _____!"

make YOUR choice

With these three words, Jesus was declaring that He had finished the work God had sent Him to do. Because of Jesus' death, I can have life! All my sins are "_____ _____ _____." (See Chart Your Course.)

MONDAY John 19:31-42

 take the challenge

Do you know what a cemetery looks like?

CHECK IT OUT

Jesus died and was buried in a tomb. (See Chart Your Course.) What are the names of the two men who carried away Jesus' body (vv. 38-39)? _____ and _____ They laid Jesus in a new _____ in a _____.

make YOUR choice

The customs of Jesus' day are different than our customs today. It was against the law for the Jews to work on the Sabbath (see Chart Your Course) so the two men had to work quickly. These two men were secret followers of Jesus. How about me? Am I a secret follower of Jesus? Do others know that I am a Christian? **Yes/ No** How do they know? _____

TUESDAY John 20:1-10

 take the challenge

Do you like mysteries?

CHECK IT OUT

When Mary, John, and Peter came to the tomb they first thought

someone had _____ Jesus' _____.

Then they remembered Jesus' words that He would "_____

_____."

make YOUR choice

Jesus came back to life! This wasn't a mystery; it was just Jesus doing what He told them He would do! Jesus came back to life and proved that He was the Son of _____. Because He lives,

I can _____.

149

WEDNESDAY John 20:11-18

 take the challenge

Do you cry when you are sad?

 CHECK IT OUT

Mary Magdalene was a close friend and follower of Jesus. As she was crying in the garden, she met Jesus and He called her by _____ (v. 16). When the disciples went back to their homes, _____ stood outside the _____. She was _____. When she looked inside, what did she see two of in the tomb?

_____

make YOUR choice

Jesus loves me and knows me by name. He wants to help me in my troubles. If I am sad, lonely, scared, or hurting, I can talk to Jesus. He knows me and loves me more than anyone else. What can I tell Jesus about today? _____

thursday John 20:19-31

take the challenge

Have you ever doubted what someone has told you?

 CHECK IT OUT

Thomas was not with the disciples when they saw Jesus for the first time. He would not believe that Jesus was alive until he saw Him for himself. Who did Jesus say was more blessed than Thomas (v. 29)? _____

_____ Why was the book of John written? The key is found in verse 31. "These are written (so) _____."

make YOUR choice

I believe that Jesus is God's Son. **Yes / No**

friday John 21:1-14

take the challenge

Have you ever been fishing?

CHECK IT OUT

The disciples were fishing and catching nothing. Then Jesus came and performed another miracle! What was it? _____

How many fish did they catch? _____ This is the third time that Jesus appeared to His disciples. He was giving them important lessons that would help them after He was gone back to Heaven.

make YOUR choice

We have a "guide book" that also helps us to know about God and His will for us. What is this Book and how often should I check it out? _____

saturday John 21:15-25

take the challenge

Have you ever said "What about THEM"?

CHECK IT OUT

Jesus told Peter that he would die for Him, and he said "What about him [John]?" Jesus told Peter that he should worry only about his own life and how he should follow Jesus, not about John. He told him to

_____ Him.

make YOUR choice

I shouldn't worry about what other people do for Jesus — just make sure I am doing what Jesus wants me to do. Am I following Him with my whole heart? **Yes / No** How can I do this daily?

_____

Chart Your Course

What's your favorite subject at school? Do you love learning new things? What kind of grades do you make in school?

Well, when Solomon was a young boy, he had a consuming passion for knowledge and wisdom! He became the literary prodigy (book worm) of his day! He studied and taught botany, zoology, business administration, poetry and theology! WOW!

Proverbs is a collection of several hundred life-changing wisdom statements that Solomon wrote down in his journals. Did you ever think of keeping a notebook of favorite quotes and sayings you hear or read? It's a great idea! TRY IT!

SUNDAY Proverbs 1:1-9

take the challenge

Do you ever think your parents' advice is outdated? Do you sometimes choose to tune them out?

CHECK IT OUT

Solomon begins this amazing book with some very wise advice. He instructs us to listen to our _____ and _____. He compares our parents' advice to a victory wreath worn on the _____ and a golden chain worn around the _____. In other words, everyone can see if you are an obedient son or daughter!

make YOUR choice

I choose to I _____ my parents and o_____ them with God's help. What can I do RIGHT NOW to honor my parents?
_____

MONDAY Proverbs 1:10-19

take the challenge

When's the last time someone you knew tempted you to get involved in something you knew wasn't right or good?

CHECK IT OUT

Can you believe that all 10 of these verses today make up only three sentences? All are about one subject: what to do when tempted to do wrong or evil. What did the sinners entice (tempt) the godly young man to do? _____

_____

What was Solomon's very simple and clear advice to the young man in

make YOUR choice

verse 10? "_____

_____"

What do I need to say "NO" to today? _____

_____

TUESDAY Proverbs 1:20 - 29

take the challenge

Can you remember a time when you knew the RIGHT thing to do, but chose the WRONG anyway?

CHECK IT OUT

This whole passage is about listening to _____

when "she" calls to us and _____ what "she"

tells us. What do some foolish people do according to verses 24-25?

Someday these fools will call on God's wisdom to help them, but God

will not _____. They will _____

God's wisdom, but will not _____ "her." Why?

(See verse 29.) Because they _____

_____

make YOUR choice

I choose to _____ to God's wisdom before I do

something _____.

WEDNESDAY Proverbs 2:1-5

take the challenge

Is it sometimes hard for you to make wise choices?

CHECK IT OUT

Complete the crossword puzzle. "My Son," if you receive (accept) my (1 across) . . . turning or inclining your (2 down) to (3 down) and your heart to (4 across) , and if you look for wisdom like you'd search for (5 across), and search for it like hidden (6 down) then you will understand or discern the (7 across) of the (8 down) and find or discover the (9 down) of God.

make YOUR choice

When I choose to have my Q_____ T_____ each day, I am being attentive to God's wisdom and His words that will change my _____. Do I love to search God's Word like I would a treasure map? **Yes / No**

thursday Proverbs 2:10-15

take the challenge

What will save or rescue me from the ways of evil or wicked people?

CHECK IT OUT

Let's find out what some very important qualities in verses 10 and 11 mean:

☐ w _ _ _ _ _ _ _ _ = knowing how to apply God's truth to your real life.

☐ k _ _ _ _ _ _ _ _ _ = what you study and learn.

☐ d _ _ _ _ _ _ _ _ _ _ _ _ = the ability to tell right from wrong and make moral choices.

☐ u _ _ _ _ _ _ _ _ _ _ _ _ _ _ _ _ = grasping or comprehending the meaning of something or someone's needs.

Place the letter of the reward this quality carries with it in the box beside each of the above: A — Will guard, preserve, protect you   B — Will be pleasant to your soul
C — Will keep, watch over, or guard you   D — Will enter your heart

make YOUR choice

Look at verses 12-15, and write down one thing I want God's wisdom to spare or save me from: _____

_____

friday — Proverbs 3:1-6

take the challenge

Have you ever noticed that God almost always includes a promise or reward with a command?

CHECK IT OUT

Match the instructions given in these verses with their God-promises.

Instruction

_____ 1. Don't let love, mercy, kindness, truth,

_____ 2. Don't forget God's law or teaching

_____ 3. Trust in God with all your heart and

_____ 4. Keep God's commands in your heart (Memorize His truths!)

Promised Blessing

A. Long life coupled with peace and prosperity (goes with two numbers)

B. Favor and a good name, reputation, or understanding with God

C. He will direct you in straight paths.

make YOUR choice

Looking at verses 5 and 6, write down a number between 1 and 10 that shows how much (with 1 being the lowest and 10 the highest): How much do I really trust God? _____ How much do I lean toward my own ways and choices? _____ How often do I acknowledge Him by getting into His Word? _____

saturday — Proverbs 3:11-18

take the challenge

Do you ever feel really blessed — like you are overflowing with happiness?

CHECK IT OUT

What is the man who finds wisdom? _____ (This word means the same as "supremely happy.") Write down three things from this passage that wisdom IS: (1) _____

(2) _____ (3) _____

What is in her (wisdom's) hands? RIGHT: _____

LEFT: _____ "All her p_____ are

p_____." (v. 18b)

make YOUR choice

I need to always remember that when I claim God's wisdom I get _____ but when I choose my own way, I get His _____ (spanking) (v. 11). I get this because God truly _____ me like His own _____.

Chart Your Course

Did you KNOW?...

That not all the proverbs were written by Solomon?

That some were written by Agur (chapter 30) and Lemuel (chapter 31)?

That the key, which unlocks all the Proverbs is found in chapter 1:7a?

"The _ _ _ _ of the _ _ _ _ is the beginning of _ _ _ _ _ _ _ _ _ _ _."

SUNDAY Proverbs 3:19-26

take the challenge

Do you ever think about awful disasters or tragedies that could happen to you or your family — and feel really afraid inside?

CHECK IT OUT

God created the earth and heavens by His _____ and

_____. Because He's in charge of everything, I do

not have to be afraid (v. 25) of _____ _____.

Verse 26a tells me why: " _____

_____."

make YOUR choice

Something I fear will happen to me or someone I love is _____

_____. I will turn this fear

over to the _____, and let Him be my

_____.

MONDAY Proverbs 3:27-32

take the challenge

What has someone asked you for – that you had – and you refused to give it to them?

CHECK IT OUT

Verses 27-30 remind us that there are people all around us — even our n_____s (v. 29) who may be in need of something we could _____ them. When I am (circle one) **greedy / gracious**, I hold on to what I have and refuse to share it. When I am (circle one) **greedy / gracious**, nothing I own is more important than helping someone else.

make YOUR choice

I choose to be g_____ today. Someone I know who could use my help is _____ _____. I will reach out to them by _____.

TUESDAY Proverbs 4:4-9

take the challenge

What's the one thing you really want to get or have more than anything else?

CHECK IT OUT

What are the two main things these verses are telling us to get or acquire? _____ and _____ Circle the one that's most important to have. Verse 8 tells us to _____ "her" and to _____ "her." If we do this, we'll be (circle one) **cursed / rich / honored and exalted ~ like a King!**

make YOUR choice

I will seek to get God's _____ each day by having a daily Q_____ T_____ in His Word and praying! Then I will use it to make _____ decisions.

157

WEDNESDAY Proverbs 4:10-19

take the challenge

Sometimes you come to a place in life where it seems like there are two paths you have to choose from before you can continue.

CHECK IT OUT

Look at the paths below, and choose some of the different characteristics of each from the phrases in today's passage. Draw a line from the characteristic to the sign that shows where it belongs.

> **wisdom way (God's Blessing!)**

long life

no stumbling

guidance in wisdom

deep

wickedness

bright like the light of dawn

> **wicked way (God's Wrath!)**

make YOUR choice

way of evil men

no sleep

good, straight paths

instruction

darkness

Which path of life will I choose to take? _____

What do I expect to find at the end of this path? _____

thursday Proverbs 4:20-27

take the challenge

Have you ever run in a race? What should your eyes be focused on when you are racing to a goal?

CHECK IT OUT

Let's focus on verses 24-27 today. Let's do a "cross-reference" on these verses. (This means we check out another verse somewhere else in the Bible that goes with or supports this passage.) Look up Hebrews 12:1,2 and read it. Do you see how these words go with Proverbs 4:24-27? In our Christian "race," we need to put away (get rid of) what? _____

_____ We need to focus straight ahead on whom? _____ We need to make sure we don't get sidetracked by swerving or turning to the _____ or _____ of God's perfect will for us (revealed in His Word).

make YOUR choice

How am I doing in my Christian race? _____

_____ What do I sometimes get my eyes on instead of Jesus? _____

_____

friday Proverbs 5:1-14

take the challenge

God has a very special person picked out for you to marry someday. But you can miss God's best for your life by falling into the trap we'll read about today!

CHECK IT OUT

This whole chapter is addressing the terrible sin of sexual impurity. It is terrible because it can affect your whole life (now and in the future) — even your marriage someday! Can you pick out three things about the sexually tempting woman of sin that might cause a guy to ruin his life?

(1) _____ (2) _____

(3) _____ Write out the warning in verses 8 and 9, and let it scare you into making a promise to yourself: "to stay sexually pure!" "_____"

make YOUR choice

The young man in these verses had come to the brink of utter ruin. Is this what I want someday? _____ What will I do to avoid sexual sin? (Circle one.)
Be careful where I go on the computer / Monitor video games I play / Don't watch bad movies and TV shows/ Watch what books and magazines I read / Stay in God's Word / Pray daily / Nothing

saturday Proverbs 5:21-23

take the challenge

Does God really see every little thing I do and know every thought I think? Whoa!

CHECK IT OUT

Write verse 21 out on the lines below:

"_____

_____

_____"

Verse 23 warns us that the sinful person will _____ for lack of (without) _____.

What a sad ending, when he had the chance to make wise, godly choices!

make YOUR choice

Knowing that God sees and knows all I think and do, I choose to walk his paths of _____ and _____.

I choose to be (circle one) **godly / ungodly / wise / foolish.**

37

Chart Your Course

Hebrews is the mystery book of the New Testament. It's actually a letter! All of the following are not known for sure, but are mysteries to us concerning the writing of this great book:

Who wrote it? When was it written? To what specific audience was it written? It was written to believers in what country?

SUNDAY Hebrews 1:1-7

take the challenge

Have you ever wished God would come down and speak to you in person?

CHECK IT OUT

This passage tells us that in the Old Testament times, God spoke to men through chosen prophets, but then He came to earth in person: the God-man, Jesus Christ! Write down at least four great things He is or did (verse 1-5): 1_____,
2_____,
3_____,
4_____,

make your choice

How can Jesus speak to me personally every day? _____
_____
_____

MONDAY 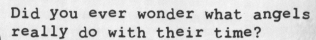 Hebrews 1:8-14

take the challenge

Did you ever wonder what angels really do with their time?

CHECK IT OUT

In verses 8-12, we see new characteristics added to the wonderful portrait of Jesus:

v. 8 - His throne will last _____.

v. 9a - He loves _____ and hates _____.

v. 9b - He has been anointed with the oil of _____

v. 10 - He laid the f_____ of the earth and created the h_____.

v. 12 - He will always r_____ (the same).

make YOUR choice

I can thank this wonderful Savior, the very Creator, for caring enough about me to send His own _____ to serve and minister to me! (Thank Him now!)

TUESDAY Hebrews 2:1-9

take the challenge

Am I really important to God? How could He care about 'little 'ole me'?

CHECK IT OUT

These verses let me know how special I am to God:

In verse 1-3, God gave us eternal s_ _ _ _ _ _ _ _.

In verse 4, God made sure we got His message by sending down (unscramble to see):

NISGS _ _ _ _ _   REDOWNS _ _ _ _ _ _ _

CREMLASI _ _ _ _ _ _ _ _   STIFG _ _ _ _ _

In verses 7-8, God raised us to a position just below the _____ and crowned us with _____ and _____. And in verse 9, Jesus even suffered _____ for me.

make YOUR choice

Say five times, "I'm special to God!" and believe it!

161

WEDNESDAY Hebrews 2:10-18

take the challenge

How do I normally handle temptation when it comes my way? Is it easier to fight it or to give in?

CHECK IT OUT

As a man on this earth, what are four things Jesus experienced that made Him better understand us humans and the things we go through?

(1) s_____ (v. 10)

(2) f_____ and b_____ (v. 14)

(3) d_____ (v. 14)   (4) t_____ (v. 18)

make YOUR choice

Since Jesus overcame temptation and never sinned, Who do I need to turn to when I'm being tempted? _____

thursday Hebrews 3:1-6

take the challenge

What do you think it means to be faithful? Do you think you are "faithful"?

CHECK IT OUT

In this passage, what Old Testament hero is Jesus compared to? _____ What character quality did both have in the mission God gave them? (Circle one.)

Faith - Compassion - Faithfulness

make YOUR choice

Jesus has been faithful to me. How can I be more faithful (loyal) to him?

_____

_____

friday Hebrews 3:7-13

take the challenge

What happens to water when it's put in the freezer for a while? How would you describe your heart relationship with God? ☐ Cold & hard ☐ Warm & tender ☐ Like Jell-o (in between!)

CHECK IT OUT

In these verses we see the dangers of not listening to God's Word and not obeying Him. What happens to our heart when this happens (v. 8)? It becomes _____ toward God. Does God bless and use a believer with a hard heart and an unbelieving spirit? **Yes / No** What does verse 13 tell me to do to stop others from going away from the Lord? "E_____ o_____ a_____ daily!"

make YOUR choice

How can I encourage (exhort) or help another Christian I know from getting a hard heart? _____

saturday Hebrews 3:14-19

take the challenge

What does the word rebellious make you think of? Do you know someone who seems to be rebellious?

CHECK IT OUT

These verses recount the story of the Israelites following Moses through the wilderness. How many years did they wander because of their unbelieving and rebellious attitudes? _____ (v.17) All those 20 years of age or older (see Numbers 14:29) were never allowed to enter God's "r __ __ __" – the Promised Land – which would have been theirs. How sad!

make YOUR choice

What special promises of God might I miss by allowing a rebellious attitude to control my heart? _____
_____.

When should I repent and make Jesus first again, according to verse 15?
_____ 163

Chart Your Course

38

Since the authorship of Hebrews is a mystery, who are the possibilities? (Circle the one you think wrote it!)

Apostle Paul? Luke? *Apollos?*

Silas? *Barnabas?* Philip?

Priscilla? **Clement of Rome?**

Do you mean a girl could have written this book? Whoa!

SUNDAY Hebrews 4:1-3, 11

take the challenge

How could the gospel message of eternal salvation be of no value to someone? Is that possible?

CHECK IT OUT

"E_____ into His r_____" is mentioned again in three verses here (and several times in verses 4-10, too). This "rest" is the secure peace we find in accepting Christ's salvation and living in His power — not having to strive by our own hard works to please God. But God's salvation ("rest") found in this letter is only of value or profit to someone if they accept it by (with) __ __ __ __ __ (v. 2).

make your choice

How am I an example of obedience to God and not disobedience?

_____

_____

How I obey by faith can lead another into God's spiritual rest!

MONDAY Hebrews 4:12-16

take the challenge

Have you ever had an operation or know someone close to you that has? How did you (they) feel after being cut open?

CHECK IT OUT

Verse 12 tells us that God's Word is "_____ and _____, and _____ than any double-edged _____."
These verses remind us that God's Word is like a surgical knife cutting deep within to get rid of the sinful places in our hearts and souls. We cannot hide anything from God's eyes.

make YOUR choice

Why is it so important for me to get into God's living Word every-day and to obey what it tells me? _____
_____

TUESDAY Hebrews 5:1-8

take the challenge

Sometimes when you hurt inside, do you wonder if there's anyone who can really understand how you feel?

CHECK IT OUT

What two names of High Priests are mentioned here? _____ and _____ Beside the statements below about their priesthood, put either an A (for Aaron) or a C (for Christ). (Some will be BOTH.)

_____ Selected from among men
_____ God's only Son
_____ Called by God alone
_____ Offered sacrifices for sins
_____ Was God's sacrifice for our sins

_____ Did not choose this honor for themselves
_____ Had to sacrifice for His own sins, too.
_____ Learned obedience through all His sufferings

make YOUR choice

If the very Son of God could learn greater obedience by suffering for me, what might God want me to learn through hard and unhappy times in my life? _____ 165

WEDNESDAY Hebrews 5:9-14

take the challenge

Do you know any grown-ups who choose to eat baby food and infant formula for each meal?

CHECK IT OUT

In the last three words of verse 11, the author rebukes these believers for being _____ _____ _____. He said when they ought to have grown enough spiritually to be (circle one) **pediatricians - hair stylists - teachers** — they were still "eating" _____ and not _____ _____ (verse 12). The more we study and learn God's Word, the more of its hard truths we understand. Then we can be _____ Christians instead of _____. (Unscramble these two words and put in the two preceding blanks: **REMUTA   ABBSEI**)

_____ _____

make YOUR choice

Mark with an X on the line below where I think I am in spiritual maturity and growth in God's Word: ____ **A tiny infant in Christ (**just saved) ____ **Toddler** (just learning the basics) ____ **Elementary** (growing in Bible knowledge) ____ **Strong in Christ** (a mature and godly person who is teaching others)

thursday Hebrews 6:1-8

take the challenge

Is it possible for a believer to hurt Jesus so much that they crucify Him on the cross all over again?

CHECK IT OUT

We are reminded again to grow out of the elementary truths of God's Word and into godly maturity. As you continue reading verses 4-8, remember who the author is writing to. (See Hebrews 3:1.) (circle one): **Unsaved hypocrites   Christian Jews   Heathen sinners**   The author is saying that when one of God's enlightened children has _____ _____ of the _____ gift of salvation and the goodness of God's _____, and then falls _____ from God and backslides into a life of sin, it is like _____ Jesus all over again!

make YOUR choice

How have I hurt or disappointed the One Who died for me by my sin or disobedience lately? _____

(Right now, tell Him you're sorry and ask for His forgiveness.)

friday Hebrews 6:9-12

take the challenge

Is there someone in your church or neighborhood who has done something extra kind for you or your family, maybe when things weren't going so well?

CHECK IT OUT

What does God never forget according to verse 10?

_____

_____

_____

make YOUR choice

I will think of one believer (God calls us "saints"!) that I can do something kind for or to and write their name here: _____.

☐ Check when accomplished!

saturday Hebrews 6:16-20

take the challenge

Have you ever been out to sea or on the lake in a big boat? When a boat or ship needs to stop and stay in one secure place for a while, what does the captain throw down into the water?

CHECK IT OUT

In verses 16-20, we can count on the fact that GOD's unchanging (immutable) promises will come true! Verse 19 tells us that this wonderful _ _ _ _ is an _____ for our _____ _____, and Jesus is our Captain! According to verse 18, what is it impossible for God to do? _____

make YOUR choice

What is one thing Jesus has promised me that I can count on and hope in?

_____

_____ 167

wk. 39

Chart Your Course

Jesus is GREATER

This exciting book shows lots of ways Jesus is greater!

than →

the prophets

the angels

Moses

the lamb sacrifices

the high priests

Joshua

SUNDAY   Hebrews 7:1-10

take the challenge

CHECK IT OUT

Most names have special meanings. Do you know what your name means?

This is a very unique passage in the Bible. Jesus is being compared here to a mystery priest in the Old Testament named M_____. He was not only a priest, but also the _____ of _____. His name and title had two different meanings, according to verse 2. Unscramble the words below to find out his name meanings: "King of _____" and "King of _____"

CEPEA and THEEGSNUISSOR

make YOUR choice

Jesus is my King of _____ and _____! I can trust Him with my heart and my life!

MONDAY Hebrews 7:11-17

take the challenge

Do you know what a priest is? - He is a go-between-- going to God on behalf of sinful people.

CHECK IT OUT

The writer here is saying that if p_ _ _ _ _ _ _ _ _ were possible by the Old Testament order of Levite priests, then there would have been no need for a priest like M_ _ _ _ _ _ _ _ _ _ . Jesus is the Heavenly Priest that sinful people like us need: a Priest with "the _____ of an _____ life" (v. 16b). He will always be there for us!

make YOUR choice

What hurts, burdens, or sins can I take to Jesus, my High Priest, today?_____
What other person could I remember in prayer today? _____
_____

TUESDAY Hebrews 7:18-22

take the challenge

Forever is a long, long time! How many people that you love or trust will be there for you forever?

CHECK IT OUT

Color or pencil in the spaces with dots in them below to find what kind of priest Jesus Christ is (according to both verses 17 and 21).

make YOUR choice

Because Jesus is my Forever Friend, I can trust Him with _____,

WEDNESDAY Hebrews 7:23-28

take the challenge

Have you ever gone to a real trial or seen one on TV? Who does the defense lawyer defend or represent before the Judge?

CHECK IT OUT

These verses tell us how _____ - much like a defense lawyer defending his client who has been accused of some crime or sin — defends or stands up for each of us (we've all sinned!) before the Heavenly Judge, _____ the Father. Jesus can plead in our behalf, because He (circle one): **Is very intelligent!** - **Loves people so much** - **Died to pay for all our sins, then rose again**

make YOUR choice

Write out the words of verse 25, putting the word me in place of them or those, and then thank Him for His complete salvation!

_____

_____

thursday Hebrews 8:1-6

take the challenge

If your teacher at school says something several times, you know it's important to remember, don't you?

CHECK IT OUT

Well, here, the writer repeats the truth about Jesus' excellent priesthood one more time! He sums up all he has said before by telling us that (v. 1) we have a _____ _____ Who is (circle one) - **sitting - standing - lying** at the _____ hand of the _____ of the _____ in Heaven. In other words, Jesus is actively defending me before God the Father on a daily basis!

make YOUR choice

How many sins per day can I take to Jesus for forgiveness? _____

Why? _____

friday   Hebrews 8:7-13

take the challenge

Have you ever wondered what is meant by the Bible divisions called the Old Testament and New Testament?

CHECK IT OUT

The word testament could also be called contract or covenant. A testament or covenant is simply an agreement between God and man. The Old Testament was God's _____ with His people through Abraham and was based on obeying His laws. (See Genesis 6:18.) The _____ Testament is God's _____ with His people (including us!) through Jesus Christ and is based on believing in Him as the One Who _____ for my sins. According to verses 10-12, the New Covenant would not just be a set of commands on stone tablets, but it would be in our m __ __ __ __ and h __ __ __ __ __ .

make YOUR choice

Verse 11 says we can actually know the Lord! Do I know the Lord personally? **Yes/No** When did I come to know Him? _____

_____

saturday   Hebrews 9:1-10

take the challenge

Do you enjoy camping out? What must it have been like for the Israelites to worship God in a big tent ("tabernacle")?

CHECK IT OUT

In the word puzzle below find six things you could have found in the Old Testament tabernacle. Manna, lampstand, tablets of stone, sanctuary, gold, curtain, covenant, ark, cherubim, candlestick, table, holy place, and veil

D	N	A	T	S	P	M	A	L	H	S
L	T	G	O	L	D	T	S	N	Y	M
I	N	I	A	T	R	U	C	K	R	A
E	C	O	V	E	N	A	N	T	W	N
V	O	M	A	R	B	L	E	E	O	N
C	H	E	R	U	B	I	M	V	O	A
S	Y	R	A	U	T	C	N	A	S	E
T	A	B	L	E	T	S	A	L	H	S
O	F	S	T	O	N	E	S	N	Y	M
H	O	L	Y	P	L	A	C	E	R	A
K	C	I	T	S	E	L	D	N	A	C

make YOUR choice

What religious ceremonies or good deeds will get me to Heaven? _____ What is the only thing that will take me to Heaven? _____

171

Chart Your Course

Hebrews is a book full of warnings! The five most important are on the signs below . . .

LISTEN WHEN GOD SPEAKS! (12:25-27)

DON'T DELAY! MOVE FORWARD! (6:1-6)

DON'T KEEP SINNING! (10:26-29)

DON'T RESIST DISCIPLINE! (12:5-7)

DON'T IGNORE YOUR SALVATION! (2:1-3)

SUNDAY   Hebrews 9:11-15

take the challenge

Have you ever wondered why the Bible talks so much about blood?

CHECK IT OUT

How many names of God do you see here? (Circle one.) **2, 7, 18**

Let's list them: v. 11 - C _ _ _ _ _ _ , High P _ _ _ _ _ _

v. 14 - the e _ _ _ _ _ _ _ _ S _ _ _ _ _ _ , G _ _ , the l _ _ _ _ _ _ God

v. 15 - Christ, the m _ _ _ _ _ _ _ of the _ _ _ testament/covenant

What other very important five-letter word that carries life through our bodies do you see? B _ _ _ _

make YOUR choice

Look at verse 14. If Christ's blood has truly taken away all my sins, then I will want to "s_ _ _ _ _ _ _ t_ _ _ _ _ _ l_ _ _ _ _ _ _ _ G_ _ _ _ _ _ _"!

MONDAY Hebrews 9:16-22

take the challenge

When was the last time you had to go out, kill a little lamb and offer it to God as a sacrifice for your sins?

CHECK IT OUT

Because the life of the body is essentially in the b _ _ _ _ (if we lose too much of it we die), and sin results in death, then the payment for sin must be the death of a living being. That is why verse 22b tells us that "without _____ of _____ there is no _____" of sin. This is why animals had to be killed and sacrificed in the Old Testament worship.

make YOUR choice

WOW! My sins require that either I die or someone else die in my place. What are some sins I've committed even this week? _____
_____

TUESDAY Hebrews 9:23-28

take the challenge

Have you ever wondered what really happens after you die — and if you can ever come back?

CHECK IT OUT

How often did the high priests of the Old Testament have to enter the Most Holy Place to offer blood sacrifices for sin? _____
_____ How did Jesus do (put) away with sin forever (v. 26b)? By the _____ of _____ According to verse 27, how often can a person die? _____ After that, if they haven't accepted Christ's s _ _ _ _ _ _ _ _ (v. 28b), they will face the j _ _ _ _ _ _ _ . (v. 27)

make YOUR choice

Judgment or eternal salvation? Circle the one that awaits me at death. How do I know? _____
_____

WEDNESDAY Hebrews 10:5-10

take the challenge

Do you like to have someone tell you what to do? Did you know that God told Jesus what to do?

CHECK IT OUT

When _____ came into the _____, God the Father did not ask for or want just a s_____ or o_____ (v. 5) from Him: He wanted Jesus to give His all — His very life. What was Jesus' response to God's calling to lay down His life for the sins of the world? Write it here from verses 7 and 9: "I (have) _____ _____ _____ _____ _____, oh _____."

make YOUR choice

What do I need to say to God when He speaks to me from His Word about changing or following His will? _____
_____

thursday Hebrews 10:11-18

take the challenge

When someone does something to hurt or disappoint you, how long do you hold it against them?

CHECK IT OUT

When the Old Testament priests offered sacrifices, they could never really _____ away _____ (v. 11). But when Jesus, our New Testament priest, offered His one all-time sacrifice (Himself), He could sit down at the _____ hand of _____, because by one _____ He has made perfect (circle one)   **overnight - five years - forever**   those who are being sanctified (made holy).

make YOUR choice

What does God's Spirit say about my sins in verse 17? "Their sins and _____ I will _____ _____ _____." When God f_____ my sins, He f_____ them forever! WOW!

friday Hebrews 10:19-25

take the challenge

Do you enjoy eating tossed salad? Well – lettuce is the main veggie in salad – just like it is in today's passage!

CHECK IT OUT

The writer tells us here that since Jesus is our great High Priest Who has given us free access to God Himself through the blood He shed for us on Calvary, we are to do three important things. They all begin with "Lettuce"... well, "Let us ..." List them here:

☐ (1) "Let us _____" (v. 22).

☐ (2) "Let us _____" (v. 23).

☐ (3) "Let us _____" (v. 24).

make YOUR choice

Which one of these three things do I most need to work on? Put a check beside it.

saturday Hebrews 10:26-31

take the challenge

Will a believer who has truly come to know Jesus as Savior – and then rebels against God and turns to sin – lose his salvation?

CHECK IT OUT

According to these verses (which, remember, were being written to Jewish Christians), a believer who deliberately keeps on sinning after knowing Christ can only look forward to (circle one): **hell - God's fiery anger and judgment - happiness**. When we know Jesus as our Savior and choose to sin against Him and disobey His Word, it's almost like trampling or stomping the _____ of _____ under _____. God's punishment for sin is not a little thing. Write out verse 31:

"_____

_____"

make YOUR choice

What have I ever done that was like stepping on Jesus and hurting Him?

_____

_____

wk. 41

Chart Your Course

THE BASKETBALL HALL OF FAME

THE FOOTBALL HALL OF FAME

THE BASEBALL HALL OF FAME

This week, visit **THE BIBLICAL HALL OF FAITH!** You'll see names like: **Abraham, Abel, Noah, Enoch, Jacob, Joseph, Gideon, Samson, David, Rahab, Samuel, Moses & Isaac!**

SUNDAY Hebrews 10:32-39

take the challenge

How confident am I that God loves me and keeps me in His care?

CHECK IT OUT

Verse 35 tells us not to cast or throw away "your _____."
As we trust Him in big and small things, He keeps all His promises to us and rewards our faith. Because Jesus is coming back (v. 37) (circle one) **someday - probably never - soon,** I should be living by _____ (v. 38).

make your choice

Look at verse 39. Which category do I fit into? (Check the box that applies.)
☐ Timid, afraid, shrinking or drawing back from stepping out for God in faith.
☐ Ready to move forward for God with strong belief in His saving grace!

MONDAY Hebrews 11:1-6

If you had to define the word faith, what would you say it is?

What do we understand about the formation of the world(s), or the universe, through faith? They were

_____

_____. Name two Old Testament Bible heroes

who proved their faith (vv. 4-5): _____ and

_____

Verse 6 tells me that "_____ _____ it's

_____ to please God." How does my faith in God show?

_____

TUESDAY Hebrews 11:7-12

Lots of people take tests to measure how smart they are. But what would be a good test of how much faith you have?

Match the following Bible characters to things that evidenced or showed their strong faith:

_____ Noah

_____ Abraham

_____ Isaac & Jacob

_____ Sarah

A. Lived in tents as heirs to God's promise

B. Received strength to conceive God's promised child

C. Built an ark to save his family

D. Obeyed, leaving his home and journeying to a place he didn't know

Measure your faith quotient! Put an X on the measuring line below where you best show faith and trust in God:

| I obey God's Word! | I go when God says, "Go"! | I believe He will answer my prayers. | I give up my plans for God's. |

177

WEDNESDAY Hebrews 11:13-19

take the challenge

Hold this up to a mirror to see a good definition of "faith":

Forsaking all I trust Him.

CHECK IT OUT

Even though the Old Testament saints had to live in a tough world and didn't always see the fulfillment of God's promises, they truly looked forward to their _____ home or country (v.16). Who do you look forward to meeting in Heaven? _____

_____

make YOUR choice

How do I know I'm going to be in Heaven someday? _____

_____

thursday Hebrews 11:20-29

take the challenge

If you could be any Bible Hero of Faith, whom would you choose to be?

CHECK IT OUT

What phrase do you see at the very beginning of just about all these verses?

"_____ _____" How many times do you count this phrase in this passage? (Circle one)   **8   7   5**

Who are three Bible heroes here you liked best?

_____   _____   _____

make YOUR choice

In verse 25, Moses chose (circle one) **pleasure (fun)** - **love** - **Christ** - **sin over** (circle one) **Christ** - **pleasures of sin** - **love**. What's my choice? _____

friday   Hebrews 11:30-35

take the challenge

Have you ever known anyone or known about anyone who was tortured for their faith?

CHECK IT OUT

Pick at least eight heroes of faith — some were tortured and even killed for their faith — out of the word puzzle below and list them here:

_____

_____

_____

_____

_____

_____

_____

_____

```
K R O F R I E N P R O P H E T S
A A H O M E A Y N K B O L D H A
R H O D A V I D I T E B K D S M
A A G I D E O N I C A S P D C S
B B O X L P A L E U M A S D L O
J E P H T H A H O U T S H D S N
```

make YOUR choice

Look at verses 33-35 and write down one of these things I'd be willing to suffer for my Savior: _____

saturday   Hebrews 11:36-40

take the challenge

Did you know there have been more Christians across our world tortured and killed for the cause of Christ in the last century than all the other years of history put together?

CHECK IT OUT

Name three ways these faith heroes were tortured or martyred (verses 36-38): (1)_____

(2)_____   (3)_____

Verses 39-40 tell us that after all these faith heroes have endured, we Christians today are the fulfillment of God's promises to them!

make YOUR choice

How blessed I am to know the Christ and the eternal salvation the Old Testament Bible heroes fought for! I need to stop and thank God for all those who've given their lives for the faith!

42

One of the greatest prayer blessings in the Bible is found in the last chapter of this wonderful book. Circle all the names for God you see here:

"Now the God of Peace, Who brought up our Lord Jesus from the dead, that great Shepherd of the sheep, through the blood of the everlasting covenant, make you complete in every good work to do His will, working in you what is well pleasing in His sight, through Jesus Christ, to Whom be glory forever and ever. Amen." (13:20-21 NKJV)

SUNDAY Hebrews 12:1-6

take the challenge

Have you ever run a race before or been in a bicycle race? What kind of clothes did you wear? How close did you come to winning?

CHECK IT OUT

In order to run the Christian race well, and win heavenly rewards, you must get rid of the extras and get running toward the goal! Fill in the columns below:

GET RID OF:

☐ Every(thing) _____ _____

☐ Entangling or besetting _____

GET RUNNING:

☐ With _____ the _____ before us

☐ Have our eyes fixed on (looking to) _____, the _____ and _____ of our faith.

make YOUR choice

Check the ones you'll do today in your Christian race!

MONDAY Hebrews 12:9-13

take the challenge

Have you ever been punished or disciplined for doing something wrong or hurtful? How did it feel?

CHECK IT OUT

Verse 10b tells us that God disciplines us for our _____. Verse 11 tells us that discipline from our heavenly _____ is not too much fun (joyful) – but instead is _____ . But if we respond correctly, later on it will produce what? _____

_____

make YOUR choice

How am I responding to the discipline God brings into my life, either through parents, teachers or leaders – or through hard times? _____

TUESDAY Hebrews 12:18-24

take the challenge

Do you ever think about Heaven and what it might be like? What are you really looking forward to in Heaven?

CHECK IT OUT

These verses are comparing Moses and the Israelites' experience with God's presence and the wonderful access we have to God and Heaven today through Christ and His sacrifice on Calvary. Write down two or three things (beings) that will be part of Heaven in verse 22-24: _____

_____

_____

make YOUR choice

Do I know Jesus personally? Yes/ No Can I talk to God everyday? **Yes / No** Will I be in Heaven for sure when He calls me out of this life? **Yes / No**

WEDNESDAY Hebrews 12:25-29

take the challenge

Whom have you refused to listen to or obey when they were trying to instruct you?

CHECK IT OUT

Verse 25 tells us not to _____ to listen to God when He _____.
If we are truly listening to God and receiving His Kingdom, we will be: (vv. 28-29)
(X out the things that are not in the verses.)

make YOUR choice

HAVING GRACE
Gossiping about others
COMPLAINING
Asking for more
Worshipping and serving God
THANKFUL
Showing reverence and awe (godly fear)

How will I let God know I'm really listening to Him and His Word?
_____
_____

thursday Hebrews 13:1-8

take the challenge

How do you prove that you love someone in your life? Do you tell them, do special things for them, give them gifts, or pray for them?

CHECK IT OUT

God starts out this chapter by saying we should _____ each other like brothers, and help others who are suffering. In verse 5, He tells us to be _____ with what we have, and then He gives us three reasons why we can be content (satisfied and happy) with Him. Complete these three reasons or promises: 1) God won't ever _____ us or _____ us (v. 5b). 2) The Lord is my _____ (v. 6).
3) Jesus Christ is always the _____: y_____, t_____ and f_____!

make YOUR choice

WOW! What neat things to know about my God! I will learn to be more content, not always wanting something else, because: _____
_____

 **friday** Hebrews 13:9-14

take the challenge

Have you ever felt all alone - like no one is there for you?

CHECK IT OUT

Verses 12-13 tells us that our Savior, Jesus, when He went to die on the cross for us, had to go outside the _____ and outside the _____. He had to face the cross for us all alone. In verse 14, what do we have to look forward to someday? _____

_____

make YOUR choice

How can I suffer for Jesus in a way that He suffered for me — through lonely times? _____

_____

saturday Hebrews 13:15-21

take the challenge

Whoa! Did you know the Spirit-led writer of the letter to the Hebrew believers prayed a prayer for us today, too?

 CHECK IT OUT

On the cloud below, write out the beautiful prayer prayed for us (me!) in verses 20-21. This is one of the most wonderful prayers in the Bible.

_____

_____

_____

make YOUR choice

How will my life — the way I act and talk — be an answer to this great prayer? _____

_____

183

43

Chart Your Course

BEEN TO ANY FUNERALS LATELY?

Well, for the next week in your Quiet Time, you will be attending a funeral. This prophetic poem is named Lamentations because it is the lament or funeral dirge (sad song or eulogy) of Jeremiah the prophet over the city he had done his best to save, Jerusalem, and its captivity in Babylon. ~ This biblical poetry book actually consists of five poems, four of which are acrostic: each verse begins with a different letter of the Hebrew alphabet (22 letters), in order. In chapters 1, 2 and 4 there is one verse for each letter. In chapter 3, there are three verses for each letter. Chapter 5 has 22 verses, but not in alphabetical order.

SUNDAY   Lamentations 1:1-7

take the challenge

Have you ever moved away from a house you had lived in for a long time – to a totally new place? How did you feel when you went back to visit and saw your old house?

CHECK IT OUT

As Jeremiah looks out over the city of Jerusalem, he remembers how it was once _____ of _____, but now is a _____ city. He cries that she has become like a w_____, when she used to be a _____ of the provinces. In verse 2 we are told she had no more _____ or _____. What had happened to Judah? (v. 3) _____ _____ Why had this happened? (See verse 5b for the answer.) _____ _____

make YOUR choice

Is there something in my life that has stolen my Christian joy? _____

Is there sin or a sinful habit that I need to deal with? _____

What do I need to make right in my life? _____

MONDAY Lamentations 1:12-17a

Have you ever been in a situation – maybe at school or home – where you felt punished along with everyone else, even though you didn't really do anything wrong?

When you read these verses, realize that it is not Jeremiah talking about himself when he says "I" and "my," but it is supposed to be Jerusalem talking as if it was a person. Write down five sad words you see here that describe how the captive Jerusalem was probably feeling: _____
_____

They were looking for someone to c_____ them in verses 16 and 17. In verse 16c, we hear the sadness when we read, "My _____ are _____ because the _____ has _____."
The enemy was not only the Persian army and the Babylonians who held them captive — but also their own sin.

Isn't it wonderful to know that even when I feel everyone else has failed or forsaken me — or that no one else understands my situation, I have (check out John 15:26) the _____ of _____ to c_____ me and guide me. He can speak to my heart every time I read and study God's Word.

TUESDAY Lamentations 2:1-8

Has anything sad or bad ever happened in your life that you felt God was responsible for? Did you feel angry with God for what happened or what He allowed?

In this passage, we see that even a godly prophet like Jeremiah, who was from the Jewish nation, blamed God sometimes for the bad things that had happened. Every time the Lord is referred to here, they are saying that God had caused all the terrible things that had happened to them. How many times do you see "the Lord" (Hebrew for Adonai) or "the LORD" (Hebrew for Jehovah) or "HE" in this passage? Put the number here: _____ That's a lot, huh? The saddest thing was when they said what in verse 5a? "The Lord _____" Was God really the enemy here, or had their sin and rebellion driven them away from Him?

_____

It's not a sin to doubt or question God sometimes when we don't understand. Even Jesus, God's Son, questioned His Father on the cross when he cried, "My God, my God, WHY have You forsaken me?" But after we tell God how we are feeling, we need to bring our doubts, anger, and fear to Him and ask Him to help us trust Him. How can I trust God more? _____
_____

185

WEDNESDAY Lamentations 2:11-22

take the challenge

Have you ever seen pictures of war or a natural disaster on TV where hundreds of people were hurt and killed? How did it make you feel to see so many people suffering?

CHECK IT OUT

Now we see Jeremiah cutting back in with his own painful observations. On the lines below, write his words from verse 11. _____
_____
_____

Circle the different types of people who were suffering and dying at the hands of their captors: children, infants (nursing or suckling babies), mothers, pets, fathers, priests, policemen, women, young men, prophets, maidens ("virgins"), cattle. In verse 19b, what does Jeremiah tell them to do? _____
_____

make YOUR choice

Even in the worst of situations — situations that may have been brought on by our bad choices — we can turn to God and _____ for His mercy. When I choose wrong, (circle one) **lots of people / only I / my parents / a few friends / my enemies** - can be hurt by my sinful choices.

thursday Lamentations 3:22-33

take the challenge

Remember that even when all we see are dark clouds and pouring rain — the sun is still shining somewhere!

CHECK IT OUT

Finally! These are the verses right smack in the middle of this poem that reveal hope in the midst of the darkness! Match the following phrases with their other half. (One has 2 matches!)

_____ 1) The Lord is good . . .

_____ 2) Because of the LORD's great love and mercies

_____ 3) Though He causes (brings) grief

_____ 4) Great is . . .

_____ 5) God's compassions never fail:

A - His unfailing love

B - To those who hope in, wait on & seek Him

C - They are new every morning

D - We are not consumed

E - Your faithfulness

F - He will have (show) compassion

make YOUR choice

Several times these verses mentioned waiting on or hoping in God. What does it mean in my life to "wait" on God or to really "hope" in Him? _____
_____

186

friday Lamentations 3:40-57

take the challenge

When you find yourself going the wrong way and suffering the consequences of your sin, what do you need to do?

CHECK IT OUT

Jeremiah begs the captive Jews — captive because of their sin and rebellion — to _____ and _____ to the LORD. He says, "Let us lift up our _____ and our _____ to _____ _ in heaven and tell Him what about ourselves? "We have _____ _____ and_____."

Look at verses 52-56. What do you think Jeremiah was talking about happening to him here? Look up his story in his other book: Jeremiah 38:6-13. At one point in his ministry, he had been thrown into an empty _____ and was left to die in the mire at the bottom. But _____ had rescued him!

make YOUR choice

Sometimes I need to stop and examine myself to see where I stand with the Lord. Some of the things I might discover about my spiritual life might be: (circle one) **a sinful habit, apathy, unconcern, a specific sin, an unforgiving spirit toward someone, bitterness.** I will pray and ask God to reveal to me areas in my life that need to be confessed and repented of today.

saturday Lamentations 5:17-22

take the challenge

Do you ever feel that God or those who are supposed to love you have forgotten you?

CHECK IT OUT

Go through these six verses today and find every word that begins with an "R". Most of them will be verbs or action words. Write them in the blanks below: (Hint: The King James translation has three, while other translations may have four or five.) _____ _____ _____ _____ _____ Write down the verse that most blessed your heart today as you read. " _____ _____ _____." Praise the Lord this wonderful poem of lament ends on a positive note!

make YOUR choice

Verse 21 reminds us that there is no time in our lives — no matter how far we have gone from Him — that God will not _____ us to Himself in love. What is an area in my life in which I need God's renewal and restoration?_____

_____

Chart Your Course

Who will you follow?
Paul? Apollos?
Jesus Christ? TV?
Friends? Traditions?

SUNDAY I Corinthians 1:1-9

take the challenge

When you write a letter, how do you begin?

CHECK IT OUT

Who wrote the book of Corinthians? _____

_____ (v. 1) It was written to believers in Christ — those who've accepted Him as their Savior. He wrote it to those who were " _____ to be _____" according to verse 2.

make YOUR choice

When did I accept Christ as my Savior? _____
_____
_____

MONDAY I Corinthians 1:10 – 17

Do you have differences of opinions with other Christians?

In verse 10, Paul tells how he wants the church to get along. What did they need to do?

_____

_____

_____

How can the above help me in getting along with others? _____

_____

TUESDAY I Corinthians 1:18 – 31

Can God use just an ordinary or average person to do His work?

In verses 26 & 27, God uses the words "not many wise," "not many noble," but "the foolish" and "the weak". Find and circle these words in the word search to the right.

```
F O O L I S H
B O P S E E W
W R O A J A S
E C E L B O N
A V T F I D E
K Q U W I S E
X L T Z S I H
```

How are some ways God could use me this week? _____

_____

_____

WEDNESDAY I Corinthians 2:1-8

take the challenge

Who is the smartest person you've ever known or heard about?

CHECK IT OUT

My faith should not be based on man's wisdom but on what (v. 5)? _____

Who is a very wise Christian you know — one who seeks God's wisdom? _____

make YOUR choice

What is my faith based on? _____

_____

thursday I Corinthians 2:9 – 16

take the challenge

Do you understand and listen when God's Word is taught, or does your mind wander?

CHECK IT OUT

Verses 12-13 say that if we have received the Spirit of God (asked Jesus into our lives) we will know or understand what? _____

_____

_____. A _____

does not receive the things of the Spirit (v. 14).

make YOUR choice

As a Christian, I should have the mind of Whom (v. 16)?

_____

friday · I Corinthians 3:1-8

take the challenge

We can share the Gospel, but can we actually save anyone?

CHECK IT OUT

"I _____, Apollos _____, but God did what (v. 6)? _____ _____ _____. The people who share Christ get their reward for faithfulness (vv. 7-8) but God is the One who saves people.

make YOUR choice

Who is a person I can share Christ with this week? _____ _____ Tell a friend this week about Jesus!

saturday · I Corinthians 3:9-15

take the challenge

Who is the biggest influence on your life?

CHECK IT OUT

Our foundation is _____ (v. 11). In the shapes below, name four kinds of materials with which one can build according to these verses =

make YOUR choice

If I am building my life on Christ, whom should I look to to influence my life? Circle the ones that should influence my life:
Pastor - Television - Sunday School Teacher - Youth leader - Bad friends - Music

Loving? God-honoring
or Self-oriented?
Humble? Proud?
Fearful? Confident?
Angry? Bitter?

SUNDAY I Corinthians 3:16-23

take the challenge

How could my body be compared to a church sanctuary?

CHECK IT OUT

If we are Christians, we are the temple of _____ and the _____ of God lives or dwells in us (v. 16). Temple means God's house. Our _____ is the temple of the Holy Spirit. God sees all that we do and how we take care of our bodies.

make YOUR choice

What can I do in order to take better care of my body for God's sake? _____

_____

MONDAY I Corinthians 4:1-10

take the challenge

What are my attitudes toward my pastor, my parents, or my teachers?

CHECK IT OUT

God wants us to be _____

_____ (v. 2). We need to be more concerned about

_____'s judgments than _____'s because

God sees our hearts. He knows our motives (v. 5).

make YOUR choice

What are some changes I need to make in order to be a good

steward of all God has given me? _____

_____

TUESDAY I Corinthians 4:14-21

take the challenge

Who watches you and follows your example?

CHECK IT OUT

If a friend followed your example would they

be doing things that please God? _____

Whom was Paul sending to the Corinthian

believers to help them? _____

_____ He was a good example because

he was _____ in the Lord.

make YOUR choice

How can I be a good example? _____

_____ Why not start by being a good

example at home.

WEDNESDAY I Corinthians 5:1-13

take the challenge

Should I be close friends with a person who says they are saved and yet does things that are wrong?

CHECK IT OUT

There is sin in the church and people in the church are not dealing with it. Paul encourages them to help this one who had sinned deal with his sin so he could be brought back to Christ (v. 5). We cannot keep ourselves from sinners, but we should not be close friends with believers who are living in sin (v. 11).

make YOUR choice

What can I do to help others when they are doing wrong? _____

_____ If they do not change, what should I do?

_____

thursday I Corinthians 6:1-11

take the challenge

Is it OK to sue another believer in Christ or take them to court?

CHECK IT OUT

Paul tells them that they shouldn't take a brother to court where unbelievers will settle the dispute. This is a poor testimony and is to their _____ (v. 5). Verses 9-10 tell what the people were like before they came to Christ. List three things in verse 11 that happened when they came to Christ.

1. _____
2. _____
3. _____

make YOUR choice

How has my life changed since I came to Christ? _____

_____

friday I Corinthians 6:12-20

 take the challenge

Does God own my body?

CHECK IT OUT

Our body is the temple of

_____ _____

_____ (v. 19). God

owns you, because He bought you.

make YOUR choice

The price God paid for me was the death and suffering of Jesus Christ His Son. Answer **T** for **True** and **F** for **False** _____ Sexual sin doesn't hurt my body._____ I can do what I want with my body because no one owns it but me. _____ God owns a Christian's body. _____ I should take care of my body because it belongs to God

saturday I Corinthians 7:1-6

 take the challenge

Do you ever think about what kind of person you may marry someday?

CHECK IT OUT

A man should have his own what? _____

Each woman should have her own what?

_____. A marriage needs to be one man

and one woman connected by God for life.

make YOUR choice

Why not put my future mate on my prayer list and pray that God would keep them pure and would work in their lives? Write down three godly traits you'd like your future mate to have: (1)_____,

(2) _____, (3) _____ 195

wk- 46

Chart your course

How are your relationships with...

Friends? **Cliques?**

Kids at school? **Mom?**

Dad? Sisters or brothers?

Teachers?

SUNDAY I Corinthians 7:10-24

take the challenge

What do you think God's design for marriage is?

CHECK IT OUT

A wife is not to _____ from her husband

(v. 10) and a husband is not to do what? _____

_____ (v. 11). God's plan is for

marriage to be a life-long commitment.

make your choice

What qualities can I start developing that would help me be a good husband
or wife someday? _____

_____

MONDAY I Corinthians 7:28-34

Is it alright if I decide not to ever marry?

If a person remains single they are concerned about what _____ (v. 32)? A person who marries is concerned about the welfare of their _____ (vv. 33-34). Whether you marry or stay single the important thing is that you love the _____.

make YOUR choice

What things show I love the Lord? _____

Write down one way I will show Christ I love him today:_____

_____

TUESDAY I Corinthians 8:1-8

take the challenge

Are there many gods or just one God?

CHECK IT OUT

DOWN
1. We know that we all have or posses what (v. 1)?
2. Who should man (anyone) love (v. 3)?
ACROSS
1. If anyone loves God, he is _____ by Him (God) (v. 3.)
3. One _____ Jesus Christ (v. 6b)
4 There is _____ God (v. 6a).
5. Through (by) whom are all _____ (v. 6).

make YOUR choice

Copy verse 6 and think about how I can live in and for God today.

_____

_____

WEDNESDAY   I Corinthians 9:1-10

take the challenge

What jobs have you done that you got paid for?

CHECK IT OUT

Paul was an _____ (v. 1). He ministered in the lives of people. As a soldier gets paid for his service, and one who plants a vineyard eats of its _____, and a dairy farmer uses the _____, and even an oxen gets fed when it is working - so those who serve the Lord need to be taken care of.

make YOUR choice

What are some ways I could encourage a missionary, a youth worker, or a pastor? _____ _____ Maybe you could encourage a missionary by writing a letter to them today.

thursday   I Corinthians 9:11-18

take the challenge

When's the last time you actually shared the Gospel with someone?

CHECK IT OUT

Paul's ministry was to preach what? _____ _____ Paul did it because he loved the Lord. He did not charge for people to come and listen to him preach. Read verse 14 again. Write in your own words what Paul was saying. _____ _____ _____

make YOUR choice

In what ways can I give so others can hear the Gospel? _____ _____

friday I Corinthians 9:19-27

A runner in a marathon strives to be first. Wouldn't you like to know how to run for God?

A Christian should run the race so he may _____ _____ (v. 24). An athlete practices and runs the race for an earthly reward. But Christians run the race to obtain what (v.25)? _____ _____ Paul trains his body so that he will not become what (v.27)? _____ _____

make YOUR choice

What are some ways I can prepare to run the race for Jesus. (Write them here.) _____ _____

saturday I Corinthians 10:1-11

take the challenge

What have you complained or grumbled about lately?

The children of Israel all had the same spiritual blessings, yet they were not pleasing to God. List four areas of sin that caused them to be overthrown in the wilderness (vv. 7-10).

1 _____
2 _____
3 _____
4 _____

make YOUR choice

Do I have trouble with complaining (murmuring)? Yes/No I will confess it to God and ask a friend or my parents to help me exhibit a grateful spirit instead. What's one thing I can be grateful for today? _____

47 the Lord's Supper, worship, encouragement, spiritual gifts, spiritual instruction

the Body of Christ

Think how many parts your body has! Well, our scripture this week reminds us that Christ's church is like one big body of believers, all with different spiritual gifts to help and encourage each other to grow in their faith.

SUNDAY 1 Corinthians 10: 12-22

take the challenge

After you have done something wrong do you ever say, "I just couldn't help it"?

CHECK IT OUT

God is _____ who will not

allow temptation beyond what you can handle

but will what? _____

_____ (v. 13).

make YOUR choice

What are two ways I can overcome temptation?

(1)_____

(2)_____

MONDAY 1 Corinthians 10:23-33

take the challenge

How much of what you do in life should please yourself, and how much should please God?

CHECK IT OUT

No one should _____ his own way or good, but should look for ways to help others (v. 24).

Decode the message.

A	D	E	G	H	I	L	O	F	R	T	V	W	Y	U
1	2	3	4	5	6	7	8	9	10	11	12	13	14	15

___ ___ ___ ___ ___ ___ ___ ___   ___ ___ ___   ___ ___ , ___ ___
13   5   1   11   3   12   3   10   14   8   15   2   8   2   8

___ ___ ___ ___   ___ ___ ___   ___ ___ ___ ___ ___   ___ ___   ___ ___ ___
6   11   11   8   11   5   3   4   7   8   10   14   8   9   4   8   2

make YOUR choice

How can this scripture message help me make godly choices?

_____

_____

TUESDAY 1 Corinthians 11:1-10

take the challenge

Can you think of two people who are heroes to you?

CHECK IT OUT

In verse 1, Paul is telling the Corinthians what? _____

_____ Paul wasn't

perfect but he was saying that he was a good example to follow. Are your heroes good examples to follow?

_____ In verses 2-9 he tells them the chain of command for the family. According to verse 3, list the chain of command for the family.... The head of the man is _____. The head of the woman is

_____ . The head of Christ is _____.

make YOUR choice

Who should be the head of my family? _____

WEDNESDAY 1 Corinthians 11:11-22

take the challenge

Do you ever pass notes, fall asleep, or whisper to your friend during a church service?

CHECK IT OUT

Paul is telling them in verses 17-22 how to conduct themselves during the _____'s S_____ (sometimes called Communion). They had a meal before Communion and the rich had plenty to eat and drink. But the poor went hungry. What was Paul's reaction to their conduct (v. 22)? (Circle one.) **happy, sad, angry, afraid**

make YOUR choice

How can I improve my conduct in church? _____

_____

thursday 1 Corinthians 11:23-34

take the challenge

Do you take Communion – the Lord's Supper – when your church observes it?

CHECK IT OUT

What does the bread symbolize (vv. 23-24)? _____

What does the cup represent (v. 25)?

_____

What happened to those who took the Lord's Supper unworthily (v. 30)? _____

_____

make YOUR choice

What do I need to do before taking the bread and juice at Communion, to make sure that my heart is right with Jesus, and that I am partaking for the right reason? _____

_____

friday 1 Corinthians 12:1-11

take the challenge

Did you know that as a Christian, you have a special spiritual gift all your own?

CHECK IT OUT

Can you list at least five spiritual gifts that are in verses 8-10? _____

_____

_____

_____

Spiritual gifts were not given to be used for our own good, but to be used for the good or profit of whom (v. 7)? _____

_____

make YOUR choice

I will pray and ask God to show me what my spiritual gift is, so I can use it to help others. The spiritual gift I think I could have is: _____

saturday 1 Corinthians 12:12-20

take the challenge

How would it affect you if you lost an arm or leg?

CHECK IT OUT

Everyone is given a spiritual _____ to use. One spiritual gift is not more important than another. If the foot should say, "Because I am not an _____ I am not part of the _____" (v. 15), that is silly! Just as both your leg and arm are important to your body, each person's gift is important in the ministry of the _____.

make YOUR choice

How can I help in my church? _____

_____

203

This week get answers to the following:

Spiritual Gifts: What are they? How can I use them? What is the definition of true love? What kind of conduct should I have in church?

Chart Your Course

SUNDAY 1 Corinthians 12:21-31

Did you ever stub your toe or bump your elbow? How did that make you feel?

Just like you grab your toe when you hurt it and your

whole body feels hurt, so it should be with the body of

Christ. Read verse 26. — We should _____ with

those who _____ and _____

with those who _____.

make YOUR choice

What are some ways I can help others who are hurting or sad?

_____

College students are often forgotten. Why not send a college student you know a letter or fun care package?

MONDAY 1 Corinthians 13:1-13

Everybody talks about love, but what is true love, really?

Find the words that describe what true love is (your Bible may refer to love as charity), and write them on the hearts below:

Now pick out what love is NOT and write them in the NOT circle.

NOT

Which of these characteristics are found in my life? _____

Which one do I need to work on? _____

According to verse 13, what is the greatest gift? _____

TUESDAY 1 Corinthians 14:1-9

Do you build others up or tear them down?

We should pursue or follow after what _____ _____ (v. 1)? After love, God puts a high priority on the spiritual gift of prophesy. "Prophesy" is "the gift of proclaiming God's truth." Many pastors and preachers have this gift. The person who prophesies speaks to people for what three reasons (v. 3)? 1. _____

2. _____ 3. _____

List some ways I can be of encouragement to someone else: _____

_____

_____ 205

WEDNESDAY 1 Corinthians 14:10-17

take the challenge

Have you ever learned some words or phrases in a foreign language?

CHECK IT OUT

The gift of tongues (a gift God especially gave to the early church believers) doesn't profit anyone unless there is an interpreter. If a missionary came to your church and talked in a language no one understood, it would be of little value to anyone unless someone could interpret what he was saying. Read verse 12. All spiritual gifts should be for what purpose? _____

_____

make YOUR choice

What gifts and abilities can I use to help in my church?

_____

_____

thursday 1 Corinthians 14:18-26

take the challenge

Have you ever been in a church meeting where you were confused about what was happening?

CHECK IT OUT

Paul would rather speak _____ words that people could understand than _____ words in a tongue that they did not understand (v. 19). Some of the Corinthians were speaking in unknown languages without an interrupter and it was causing unbelievers to think their behavior was ridiculous.

make YOUR choice

What are some ways you can be orderly in church? Circle the correct ones. **Talk to my friends during the sermon - Pay attention to what the pastor or teacher is saying - Laugh during the song time - Sit still and quietly - Write notes to a friend**

friday 1 Corinthians 14:27-40

 take the challenge

Does everyone in your church or class speak all at the same time?

CHECK IT OUT

Should more than one person talk at once (v. 30)?

_____

Paul says that all things should be done how (v. 40)?

_____

make YOUR choice

When someone else is talking, what should I be doing? _____

_____

saturday 1 Corinthians 15:1-11

 take the challenge

Do you know how to share the Gospel with someone, using the Bible?

CHECK IT OUT

Paul shares with them the message that

_____ died for our _____ and

that he was buried and _____

again according to the scriptures (verses 3-4).

We do not have a dead God for He was seen by

more than_____ people (v. 6).

make YOUR choice

I can share the above message with _____.

I can do this by sharing my testimony.

Chart YOUR Course

Guess where
he is going?

SUNDAY 1 Corinthians 15:12-19

take the challenge

How do you know Christ has risen from the dead?

CHECK IT OUT

If it is not true that Christ arose from the dead, we are not forgiven and are the most unhappy people in the world. Look back in 1 Corinthians 15:6–8 and make a list of the people who had seen Jesus after He rose from the dead. 1. _____

2. _____   3. _____

4. _____

make YOUR choice

Many witnesses saw Christ, proving that He had risen. Because Christ rose, someday all the believers in Christ will also rise again! That includes ME, if I am saved! Will I rise again? **Yes / No**

MONDAY 1 Corinthians 15:20-28

How did sin come into our world?

For as in _____

all die, through Christ all were

made _____ (v. 22).

Jesus Christ defeated sin. Through Christ

all men were made alive!

Do I have eternal life in Christ? _____

If I do, who can I share Christ with this week? _____

Why not create a gospel tract and give it to someone.

TUESDAY 1 Corinthians 15:29-38

Which of your friends influences you for good and which ones for bad?

Sometimes we think we can hang out with wrong

friends and still be OK. Write out verse 33 here:

_____

_____

_____

_____

Who you make friends with will determine what you will become

like. What changes do I need to make in my friendships?

_____

209

WEDNESDAY 1 Corinthians 15:39-50

take the challenge

You definitely have a natural body but do you have a spiritual body?

CHECK IT OUT

List the characteristics of the natural body:

It is sown in:
_____

It is sown in:
_____

It is sown in
_____

It is sown as a:
_____

List the characteristics of the spiritual body:

Raised in:
_____ (v. 42)

Raised in:
_____ (v. 43a)

Raised in:
_____ (v. 43b)

Raised as a:
_____ (v. 44)

make YOUR choice

My earthly (natural) body will be buried, but it will be resurrected as a spiritual body that will live for eternity! Which is better? _____

_____

thursday 1 Corinthians 15:51-58

take the challenge

Do you know what "the Rapture" is

CHECK IT OUT

Christ will come back in the clouds to take those who have believed in Him up to Heaven. This is known as "the Rapture". The first thing that will happen is that we will be changed. How fast will that happen (v. 52)? _____

What will happen when the trumpet sounds (v. 52)?

_____ .

make YOUR choice

List three things that we should be doing until the Rapture happens (v. 58).

(1)_____,

(2)_____,

(3)_____

friday 1 Corinthians 16:1-12

take the challenge

Have you ever wondered how much of your money you should give to God?

CHECK IT OUT

Paul asked the Corinthians to do what on the first day of every week (v. 2)? _____

_____

He realized some had more than others and asked them to _____ according to the income God had given them.

make YOUR choice

Has God given me some money that I can use to help my church or someone in need? **Yes/ No** _____ If you answered yes, then write here how you will give it? _____

saturday 1 Corinthians 16:13-24

take the challenge

What are some characteristics God wants in a Christian's life?

CHECK IT OUT

List the four characteristics God wants us to have in our

lives (v. 13): (1)_____,

(2) _____, (3) _____,

(4)_____ How are they to be done

(v. 14)? _____

make YOUR choice

How can you show your love to someone today? _____

_____ Why don't

you try making an "Encouragement Card" for someone.

211

Chart Your Course

With whom should we share Christ?

Friends?
Neighbors?
Enemies? Family?
Schoolmates?
Teachers?

SUNDAY 2 Timothy 1:1-7

take the challenge

Have you ever thought about sharing the Gospel with a friend, and then felt too afraid to do it?

CHECK IT OUT

What has God NOT given us (v. 7)?

_____

But He HAS given us what three things (v. 7)?

(1) _____, (2) _____,

(3) _____

make your choice

What can I do to overcome fear in my life? _____

_____

MONDAY 2 Timothy 1:8-12

take the challenge

What about your life and actions? Do they show you trust God?

CHECK IT OUT

God has called us, not according to our abilities but according to His own what (v. 9)?

_____ and _____

Paul was not afraid to share Christ because he knew what (v. 12)? _____

_____

make YOUR choice

Paul's trust was in God. Where is my trust? (Circle them)

Mom and Dad - Money - Friends - TV - Church Books - Jesus - Pastor - Bible - School teachers Neighbors

TUESDAY 2 Timothy 1:13-18

take the challenge

What kind of friend are you? How would your friends rate you?

CHECK IT OUT

Paul had some friends that left him. But he had one friend who stayed with him and encouraged him. What is the name of Paul's faithful friend (v.16)? _____

What did he do for Paul? _____

make YOUR choice

What type of friend am I? (Check the ones that apply.)
____ Try to help ____ Make fun of others ____ Listen attentively
____ Tell Lies ____ Want my own way ____ Possessive
What are some ways I can be a better friend?
_____

213

WEDNESDAY 2 Timothy 2:1-7

take the challenge

Do you share what you have learned through your Quiet Time with others?

CHECK IT OUT

Paul is telling Timothy that he needs to share what Paul has taught him to whom? _____ men (v. 2) And they should

teach whom (v. 2)? _____ Who are the people

in your life that are teaching you about Christ? _____

_____

make YOUR choice

What are some ways I can share what God is teaching me with

others? _____

_____

thursday 2 Timothy 2:8-14

take the challenge

Can God deny or disown Himself?

CHECK IT OUT

Across
1. If we suffer or endure suffering, we shall also _____ with Him (v. 12).
2. Remember _____ Christ (v. 8).
3. He abides (remains) _____ (v. 13).

Down
4. Jesus _____ was raised from the dead (v. 8).
5. If we are dead (died) with Him, we will _____ with Him (v. 11).

make YOUR choice

What have I done lately that hurt Jesus? _____

_____ But this does not change His (circle one)

anger - sorrow - love for me.

friday 2 Timothy 2:15-19

What do you like to talk about with your friends?
Sports? Movie stars? Fashion? Video games? Shopping? Other people?

Verse 16 tells us to avoid or shun what? _____

Two men who had not been careful and left the truth of God's Word were

H_____ and P_____. What a good

thing to be assured that (v. 19b): _____ _____

_____ _____ _____

_____ _____ We need to make sure that our

conversations honor God. We want to encourage others with our words, not

tear them down!

What kind of friends do I spend the most time with? _____

_____ What do we talk about? _____

_____

saturday 2 Timothy 2:20-26

What characteristics do you think are important in order to be a good friend?

What are we to flee (run from)? _____

_____ But we are to follow (pursue) what four

things? 1. _____ 2. _____

3. _____ 4. _____

Out of what kind of heart (v. 22)? _____

_____

I should not strive or quarrel with others but treat them how (vv. 24-25)?

_____

_____

Be a true friend to someone who needs to know Jesus.

wk.

51

In this week's Quiet Time we will see examples to follow. Whose example should I be following?

Sunday school teachers? Youth leaders? Friends? TV? Internet? Parents? Pastor? Movie Stars? Club Leaders? Jesus?

chart YOUR course

SUNDAY 2 Timothy 3:1-7

take the challenge

Are there any types of people we should avoid (stay away from)?

CHECK IT OUT

There are evil people who would like to lead others away from the truth of God's Word. Some even have lots of education, where they are always learning but never coming to the _____

_____(v.7)?

make YOUR choice

Circle **T** for True and **F** for False. **T / F** There are evil people all around us. **T / F** I need to be careful that I check out what people are saying and see if it is true according to God's Word. **T / F** Some people may know many things, and still not know God.

216

MONDAY 2 Timothy 3:8-12

take the challenge

Whose example are you following?

CHECK IT OUT

Paul gave Timothy a good example to follow in the characteristics below:
(Find these words in the puzzle.)

Persecutions

Teaching	Patience
Doctrine	Love
Purpose	Godly
Endurance	

```
K S N O I T U C E S R E P E T S
L A H F E N D U R A N C E D H Y
O H O I A V I E N I R T C O D L
V A P A T I E N C E A S P D S D
E B O T L P U R P O S E S D S O
J E P H T H A P T E A C H I N G
```

make YOUR choice

How can I be a good example to others?

_____

_____

TUESDAY 2 Timothy 3:13-17

take the challenge

How will the Word of God make you a better person?

CHECK IT OUT

List the things (v. 16) that all scripture is profitable for:

1. _____

2. _____

3. _____

4. _____

make YOUR choice

What are some things that scripture can help me do?

_____

_____

WEDNESDAY 2 Timothy 4:1-4

take the challenge

Do you want to hear what God is saying to you?

CHECK IT OUT

Paul tells Timothy to preach what (v. 2)? _____

He should be prepared to preach when (v. 2)? _____

How should he preach (v. 2)? _____

Even though people may not want to hear the truth, we need to continue to tell them.

make YOUR choice

Whom do I need to tell about Jesus? _____

_____ Why not put them on your prayer list and pray for them each day?

thursday 2 Timothy 4:5-8

take the challenge

What kind of rewards will there be in Heaven?

CHECK IT OUT

Paul knows that the end of his life is near. What three things in verse 7 has Paul accomplished?

(1) _____, (2) _____,

(3) _____ In verse 8 Paul says that there is laid up (in store) what? _____

_____

make YOUR choice

How can I be faithful to God? _____

_____

_____

friday 2 Timothy 4:9-15

take the challenge

What should you do when you feel like quitting?

CHECK IT OUT

Paul wanted Timothy to come to him and bring

_____ (v. 11) with him. What was

Alexander's job?_____

Why did Paul say to beware of him?_____

_____

make YOUR choice

What type of people should I stay away from? _____

_____

saturday 2 Timothy 4:16-22

take the challenge

What would you do if all your friends deserted you?

CHECK IT OUT

At Paul's first defense (trial or answer) no one

stood by him, but all _____

him (v.16). _____ _____ stood with

Paul and strengthened him (v. 17). The result was

that all the Gentiles heard the gospel message.

make YOUR choice

Who will never leave me? _____

Look up Hebrews 13:5 for this promise in writing from God!

wk

52

Chart Your Course

This week we are going to look at two "minor" (their messages are small compared to the "major" prophets like Isaiah and Jeremiah) prophets and their powerful messages. Both spoke to different audiences with different goals in mind. Let's look at the difference in their messages:

	NAHUM	MALACHI
Time written:	630 BC, about 150 yrs. after Jonah	About 435 BC
Probably knew:	Jeremiah, Habakkuk, Zephaniah	Ezra & Nehemiah
Name meaning:	"The comfort of Jehovah"	"The messenger of Jehovah"
Prophesied to:	Mostly the natives of Nineveh	The Israelites (Jews) who had returned from captivity in Babylon
Theme:	God rules & God will judge!	The sinful priests, the sinful people, the faithful few

SUNDAY Nahum 1:1-7

take the challenge

When you think of Nineveh, whom do you usually think of? (Does a whale come to mind?)

CHECK IT OUT

Remember when all the Ninevites repented and turned to God after Jonah's message of wrath? Now, 150 years later, we find these Assyrians just as wicked and cruel as they had originally been. This time there would be no repenting! Look at verses 7 and 8 and see the contrast here: "The _____ is _____, a _____ in the day of _____. He knows and cares for those who trust in Him for refuge. BUT with an _____ _____ He will make an end of Nineveh and His enemies will be overcome by darkness!" ~ Archaeologists have discovered that the Tigris River overflowed, carrying away part of their 100-foot high wall. This made it easy for the enemy troops of Medo-Persia to enter and destroy the city.

make YOUR choice

Do I really believe that "the Lord is GOOD"? _____ All the time? _____ Even when He has to punish people for their sinfulness? _____ And even when nothing seems to be going right? _____ I can _____ _____ God in any situation, because He knows what is best for me.

MONDAY Malachi 1:6-14

take the challenge

Have you ever felt impressed to give a special offering to the Lord, and then decided to spend most of your money on something you wanted instead – and just gave a few cents in the offering plate?

CHECK IT OUT

In order to understand the important message Malachi was trying to get across to these Jews who had wandered away from His commands and truths, turn back in your Bible to Leviticus (third book of Bible) and check out 1:3 and 1:10 to see what kind of animal sacrifices God required from His worshippers. They were to be "a (circle one) male / female - without what?_____ " This means the animal was to be perfect in every way. Now look at verses 8 and 13 in our passage today, and tell me what kind of sacrifices were being offered to God: _____

make YOUR choice

God wants a pure offering. He wants my best not my worst — or even something in between. What am I giving God that is really a sacrifice (of my time, of my energy, of my money, of myself) — that truly costs me something? _____ Remember, He sacrificed His life for me on the cross of Calvary.

TUESDAY Malachi 2:1-2 and 7-9

take the challenge

What do you appreciate most about the Pastor of your church?

CHECK IT OUT

In this passage, Malachi is addressing the priests or God-appointed pastors of the people. Notice the interesting phrase in verse 2, where God says to these priests who were not glorifying His name, "I will send a _____ upon you, and I will _____ your _____."
Here were the priests who were supposed to be blessing God's people and sharing God's Word with them. The end of verse 7 says the priest was supposed to be "the _____ of Whom? _____
_____ But what had they done instead (v. 8)? _____

make YOUR choice

God has given me a pastor at my church to teach me more about His truths from His Word and to help me know God's blessing and guidance in my life. How can I thank him this week for letting God use him to minister to so many others, as well as myself? _____

WEDNESDAY Malachi 2:10-16

take the challenge

What kind of home do you live in? Are you from a broken home? Do your parents ever fight? What is God's will for husbands and wives?

CHECK IT OUT

There were two specific issues that Malachi addressed in these verses. The first is in verses 11-12, where he says that the Jews had been marrying (circle one) foreign ungodly mates / godly Jewish mates. The second issue is one we face a lot in today's world. In verse 16, what does God say He hates? _____ _____ and violence or abusive behavior In verses 13 — 15, he shares that marriage is the binding covenant or agreement between a man and woman which makes them one, and it is never meant to be broken.

make YOUR choice

Someday when I am old enough to get married, I want to make sure I date and marry only a _____ mate and that I marry for _____! (It wouldn't be a bad idea at all to make this a prayer request that I pray for every week!)

thursday Malachi 3:1-6

take the challenge

Did you know that Jesus' second coming is prophesied in the Bible eight times as much as His first coming (as a baby in a manger)?

CHECK IT OUT

Today we see Malachi foretelling the coming of the Messiah. Some of his prophecies refer to Christ's first coming, but some also describe His second coming — something we are still looking forward to! How will Jesus come according to verse 1? _____ What will he be like (v. 2) _____ This is referring to His brightness and righteousness! Circle the people He will judge when He returns as King (v. 5): missionaries; adulterers; tax collectors; sorcerers; those who are dishonest; people who swear; doctors; cheaters; those who oppress or cheat widows, orphans or immigrants (strangers, aliens)

make YOUR choice

If I knew Jesus was going to come back today, what would I change about the way I speak or act? _____ _____

friday Malachi 3:7-12

take the challenge
Did you know that folks can actually ROB GOD??

CHECK IT OUT

What had these people gone (turned away) from? _____
_____ But God challenged them: "_____ unto Me and
I will _____ unto _____." One of the ways He encouraged
them to return was in the giving of their tithes (10% of what they earned) and
offerings (any amount as a love gift to God). What did He say they would see
Him do if they began to give unselfishly to Him and His house again?
(See v. 10.) _____

make YOUR choice

Look up James 4:8a and cross-reference it with today's verse 7b. How are
these verses alike? _____
So what am I doing today to get nearer — to get closer — to God?
_____
How am I doing at giving God at least 10% of all the money I get?
_____

saturday Malachi 3:16–4:3

take the challenge
Who are your very best friends? Are they
kids who like to talk about the Lord,
the Bible and what God is doing in their
lives? Do you feel comfortable to pray
with them about things?

CHECK IT OUT

What did those folks do who "feared [respected] the LORD"? _____
_____ Who heard and listened to their conversation?
_____ A "book of _____" (like a scrapbook,
journal, diary or family photo album) was written in God's presence
(maybe at the place of worship) about or for those who _____
the _____ and _____ His _____." What did God
say about those who honored (feared or revered) His name (v. 2)? "The
_____ of _____ will rise with _____
in His _____." Do you think this could be talking about Jesus
Christ, God's Son (Sun?) — the Light of the World who brought eternal
healing to all who would trust Him? **Yes / No**

make YOUR choice

Write out the words God says about His own in verse 17a: "They _____
be _____ _____ _____ day _____
_____." If I am God's own child, then that means I am His. WOW! God
treasures me and wants to bless and use me for His glory. I am His! (Maybe you
could write it on a card and put it up where you'll see it everyday!) 223

tO wOrd OF LiFe OLyMPiaN MeMbeRs

So that all club members will be on the same passages, the following dates correspond to the weekly passages. These dates are also used for the adult and teen Quiet Times and the daily Word of Life Radio broadcasts.

Wk 1	Aug 27-Sep 2	Ps 1:1-7:8	Wk 27	Feb 25-Mar 3	John 5:15-6:58
Wk 2	Sep 3-Sep 9	Ps 7:9-11:7	Wk 28	Mar 4-Mar 10	John 6:59-8:24
Wk 3	Sep 10-Sep 16	Ps 12:1-17:15	Wk 29	Mar 11-Mar 17	John 8:25-10:13
Wk 4	Sep 17-Sep 23	Ps 18:1-21:13	Wk 30	Mar 18-Mar 24	John 10:14-12:11
Wk 5	Sep 24-Sept 30	Ps 22:1-25:22	Wk 31	Mar 25-Mar 31	John 12:12-14:14
Wk 6	Oct 1-Oct 7	Eph 1:1-2:22	Wk 32	Apr 1-Apr 7	John 14:15-16:33
Wk 7	Oct 8-Oct 14	Eph 3:1-4:32	Wk 33	Apr 8-Apr 14	John 17:1-19:22
Wk 8	Oct 15-Oct 21	Eph 5:1-6:24	Wk 34	Apr 15-Apr 21	John 19:23-21:25
Wk 9	Oct 22-Oct 28	Esther 1:1-5:14	Wk 35	Apr 22-Apr 28	Prov 1:1-3:18
Wk 10	Oct 29-Nov 4	Esther 6:1-SofS 6:3	Wk 36	Apr 29-May 5	Prov 3:19-5:23
Wk 11	Nov 5-Nov 11	Titus 1:1-Phil 25	Wk 37	May 6-May 12	Heb 1:1-3:19
Wk 12	Nov 12-Nov 18	Rev 1:1-2:29	Wk 38	May 13-May 19	Heb 4:1-6:20
Wk 13	Nov 19-Nov 25	Rev 3:1-6:8	Wk 39	May 20-May 26	Heb 7:1-9:10
Wk 14	Nov 26-Dec 2	Rev 6:9-10:11	Wk 40	May 27-June 2	Heb 9:11-10:31
Wk 15	Dec 3-Dec 9	Rev 11:1-14:7	Wk 41	Jun 3-Jun 9	Heb 10:32-11:40
Wk 16	Dec 10-Dec 16	Rev 14:8-17:18	Wk 42	Jun 10-Jun 16	Heb 12:1-13:25
Wk 17	Dec 17-Dec 23	Rev 18:1-20:6	Wk 43	Jun 17-Jun 23	Lam 1:1-5:22
Wk 18	Dec 24-Dec 30	Rev 20:7-22:21	Wk 44	Jun 24-Jun 30	1 Cor 1:1-3:15
Wk 19	Dec 31-Jan 6	1 Kings 1:15-11:13	Wk 45	Jul 1-Jul 7	1 Cor 3:16-7:9
Wk 20	Jan 7-Jan 13	1 Kings 11:41-18:16	Wk 46	Jul 8-Jul 14	1 Cor 7:10-10:11
Wk 21	Jan 14-Jan 20	1 Kings 18:17-22:40	Wk 47	Jul 15-Jul 21	1 Cor 10:12-12:20
Wk 22	Jan 21-Jan 27	2 Kings 1:1-5:16	Wk 48	Jul 22-Jul 28	1 Cor 12:21-15:11
Wk 23	Jan 28-Feb 3	2 Kings 5:17-9:37	Wk 49	Jul 29- Aug 4	1 Cor 15:12-16:24
Wk 24	Feb 4-Feb 10	2 Kings 13:14-23:3	Wk 50	Aug 5-Aug 11	2 Tim 1:1-2:26
Wk 25	Feb 11-Feb 17	John 1:1-3:12	Wk 51	Aug 12-Aug 18	2 Tim 3:1-4:22
Wk 26	Feb 18-Feb 24	John 3:13-5:14	Wk 52	Aug 19-Aug 25	Nah 1:1-Mal 4:6